UNITED STATES

in Pictures

Tom Streissguth

TF CB
Twenty-First Century Books

Contents

Lerner Publishing Group realizes that current information and statistics quickly become out of date. To extend the usefulness of the Visual Geography Series, we developed www.vgsbooks.com, a website offering links to up-to-date information, as well as in-depth material, on a wide variety of subjects. All of the websites listed on www.vgsbooks.com have been carefully selected by researchers at Lerner Publishing Group. However, Lerner Publishing Group is not responsible for the accuracy or suitability of the material on any website other than www.lernerbooks.com. It is recommended that students using the Internet be supervised by a parent or teacher. Links on www.vgsbooks.com will be regularly reviewed and updated as needed.

Website address: www.lernerbooks.com

Twenty-First Century Books
A division of Lerner Publishing Group, Inc.
241 First Avenue North
Minneapolis, MN 55401 U.S.A.

web enhanced @ www.vgsbooks.com

CULTURAL LIFE

44

▶ Religion. Literature. Art and Media. Music.
Sports. Food. Holidays and Festivals.

THE ECONOMY

56

▶ Services. Manufacturing and Trade. Mining and
Energy. Agriculture. Forestry and Fishing.
Transportation and Tourism. Communications.
The Future.

FOR MORE INFORMATION

Library of Congress Cataloging-in-Publication Data

Streissguth, Thomas, 1958–
       United States in pictures / by Tom Streissguth.
          p.   cm. – (Visual geography series)
       Includes bibliographical references and index.
       ISBN 978-0-8225-8567-1 (lib. bdg. : alk. paper)
       1. United States—Juvenile literature. 2. United States—Geography—Juvenile literature. 3. United
States—History—Juvenile literature. 4. United States—Pictorial works—Juvenile literature. I. Title.
E156.S77 2008
973–dc22   2006100679

Manufactured in the United States of America
2 3 4 5 6 7 – BP – 13 12 11 10 09 08

INTRODUCTION

The United States of America spans central North America from the Atlantic to the Pacific oceans. Native American peoples were the first to populate the continent. The modern nation began as Spanish, French, and British explorers arrived from Europe. British colonists founded colonies in the seventeenth century along the Atlantic seaboard. These colonies won their independence as the United States of America in 1783. The nation grew as new states joined the union.

The United States spread westward as far as the Pacific Ocean coast. Pioneers settled land from the Canadian border in the north to the Rio Grande and the Gulf of Mexico in the south. Alaska, a territory lying north and west of Canada, and Hawaii, an island group in the Pacific Ocean, became states in the middle of the twentieth century. The United States also owns overseas territories, including Puerto Rico and Guam.

The United States attracted immigrants from around the world. In the nineteenth century, the nation's eastern urban areas swelled as

European settlers came to work in factories. Open land and gold and silver mining drew pioneers to the Great Plains and the Rocky Mountains. In the late twentieth century, Latin America and Asia became the leading sources of new immigrants.

With plentiful fertile land, the United States developed into the world's leading agricultural nation. For many years, U.S. farmers have raised enough food to meet domestic demand and for export. U.S. industries—from automaking to high technology—compete in markets around the world. For decades the United States has produced more goods each year than any other nation. Its people enjoy one of the highest standards of living in the world.

Since the early 1990s, the United States has also emerged as the world's lone superpower. The country's political clout is present on every continent. The U.S. military leases naval, land, and air bases in dozens of countries. U.S. policy plays a vital role in many of the world's ongoing conflicts.

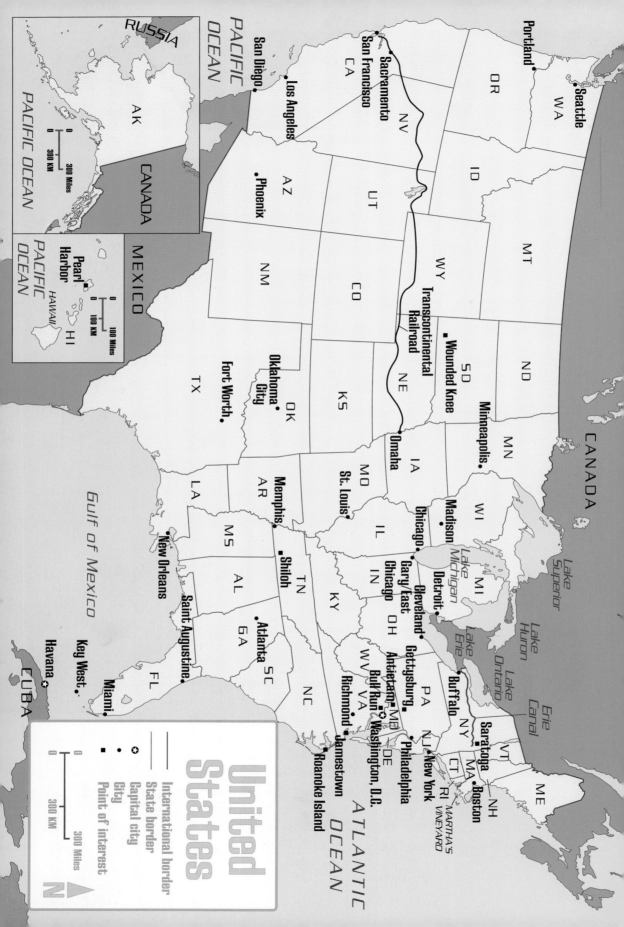

The United States has also become a technological leader. U.S. companies make computers and the software to run them. The Internet began in the United States as a communications system for the military and at universities. American movies, books, music, and art have all found a global audience.

Compared to most other nations, the United States is militarily, politically, and economically strong. Yet serious issues are testing the nation's leaders. In many cities, crime and poverty remain problems. A wave of newcomers, many of them living in the United States without permission, has sparked a bitter debate over immigration. The growth of cities and industry is damaging the natural environment. The United States also is involved in tough business competition with other nations, particularly China.

The United States has strained relations with some foreign governments. Many societies resist its worldwide political, military, and cultural strength. For that reason, U.S. leaders are trying to strike a balance between serving the national interest and keeping good relations with foreign nations. Achieving this goal is vital to continuing prosperity within U.S. borders.

THE LAND

The United States is the fourth-largest country in the world, after Russia, Canada, and China. The total area of the fifty states is nearly 3.8 million square miles (9.8 million square kilometers). The United States borders Canada in the north. To the south are Mexico and the Gulf of Mexico. Other possessions include Guam and American Samoa in the Pacific Ocean. In the Caribbean, the United States includes the Commonwealth of Puerto Rico, the U.S. Virgin Islands, and Navassa Island. These offshore territories add about 12,000 square miles (31,080 sq. km).

Topography

The United States has a varied landscape, with mountains, plains, deserts, and low-lying coastal regions. The mainland can be divided into six main geographical regions.

ATLANTIC COASTAL PLAIN The narrow Atlantic Coastal Plain borders the Atlantic Ocean from the state of Massachusetts southward to Florida. The

oceanfront consists of wetlands (low, wet areas), river estuaries (where rivers meet the ocean), and small islands. The estuaries form natural ports such as New York City, Baltimore, Maryland, and Newport, Virginia.

The northeastern United States has the highest population density of any major region. It includes a long corridor of major population centers, from Boston to Washington, D.C. Suburbs sprawl from the city centers to the surrounding areas, greatly enlarging the urban area.

Along the coastal plain, fertile soils produce several major crops. Farmers grow much of the nation's citrus fruits in central Florida. In other sections of the Coastal Plain, however, the soil is naturally poor or nearly sterile from years of intensive farming.

APPALACHIAN MOUNTAINS The Appalachians rise west of the Atlantic Coastal Plain. These low, rounded highlands run from eastern Canada to northern Alabama. The Green Mountains of New Hampshire and the Catskill Mountains of New York belong to the northern Appalachians.

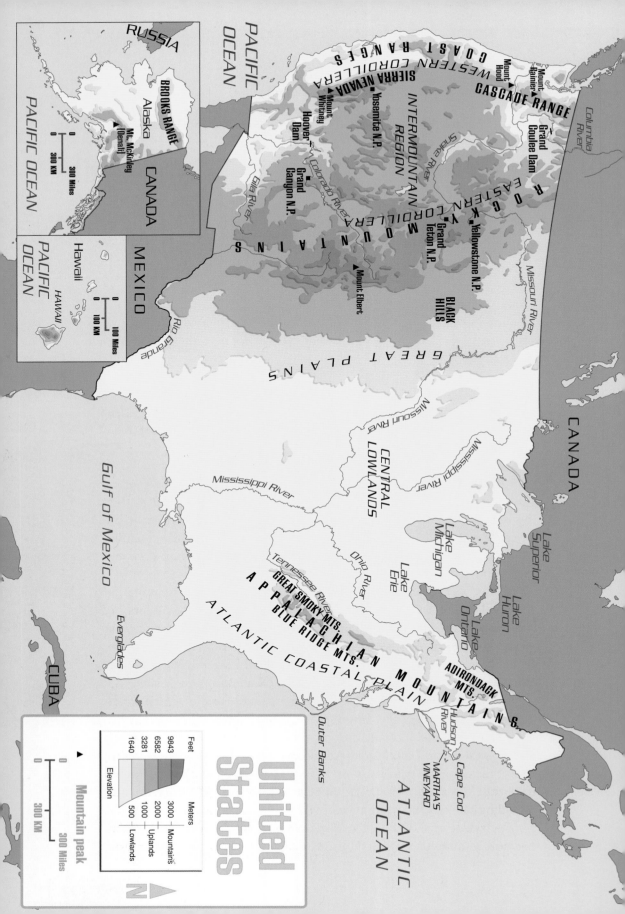

The Blue Ridge Mountains rise in northern Virginia. The Great Smoky Mountains straddle the border between North Carolina and Tennessee.

Appalachian farmers raise poultry, corn, tobacco, potatoes, and wheat in the valleys between the ranges. Miners extract much of the nation's coal from the region's underground deposits.

CENTRAL LOWLANDS The Central Lowlands lie west of the Appalachians. Thousands of years ago, glaciers inched across the northern half of this region. The mountains of ice sculpted the terrain and carved river valleys. Most of the lowlands are flat or gently rolling plains. Elevations do not exceed about 2,000 feet (610 meters) above sea level.

Glacial basins hold thousands of lakes, including the Great Lakes of Ontario, Huron, Erie, Michigan, and Superior. These make up the largest group of freshwater lakes in the world. Farther south, across the states of Iowa, Illinois, Indiana, and Ohio, the glaciers deposited large tracts of fertile soil.

GREAT PLAINS The Great Plains, a largely treeless region west of the Central Lowlands, reaches 4,000 feet (1,219 m) above sea level. Elevation rises gradually from east to west. The Great Plains extend from Texas northward into Canada and from the Mississippi River valley west to the Rocky Mountains.

Vast herds of American bison (buffalo) fed on the native grasses of the plains until the late nineteenth century. Settlers from the east then plowed the soil to plant wheat. This crop, along with the meat provided by cattle and sheep, made the United States a leading agricultural nation. But drought and soil erosion in the plains have led to poor harvests and crop failures.

INTERMOUNTAIN REGION The Intermountain Region consists mainly of rocky plateaus and bowl-shaped basins. These features are common in western Colorado, Arizona, Nevada, and Utah. In some places, rivers have eroded the plateaus to form buttes (isolated, flat-topped hills) and steep canyons. Long, low mountain ranges rise from the desert basins. The southwestern deserts are the driest and hottest areas of the United States.

CORDILLERA The Cordillera is a mountain system between the Great Plains in the east and the Pacific coast in the west. The Rocky Mountains, part of the eastern Cordillera, run north to south from Alaska and Canada to Mexico. This range boasts some of the tallest peaks in North America, including Mount Elbert, which reaches 14,433 feet (4,399 m) in Colorado.

The western Cordillera includes the Coast Ranges, the Sierra Nevada, and the Cascades. Several major cities—including Portland,

Oregon, and Sacramento, California—lie in the valleys between these mountains. The Sierra Nevada features Mount Whitney. At 14,494 feet (4,418 m), it is the highest peak of the mainland United States. The Cascade Range includes Mount Hood, Mount Rainier, and a number of active volcanoes.

ALASKA AND HAWAII Alaska, the nation's largest state, lies 500 miles (805 km) northwest of the state of Washington. The Brooks Range, the northernmost section of the Rocky Mountains, rises above permanently frozen, treeless ground. The Coast Ranges of the Western Cordillera reach into southern Alaska. Mount McKinley (Denali), the highest peak in North America, reaches 20,320 feet (6,194 m).

Hawaii lies about 2,400 miles (3,862 km) southwest of the mainland. This archipelago (island group) includes eight major volcanic islands and more than one hundred islets. Some of these lush, tropical islands are actually large deposits of coral, marine animals that form large underwater reefs. The largest Hawaiian island, known as the island of Hawaii, is the exposed top of an active volcano.

Rivers

Waterways in the United States are vital to transportation, irrigation, and hydropower (energy produced from running water). The nation's major river systems are the Hudson, the Mississippi, the Ohio, the Colorado, and the Columbia rivers.

The Hudson and the Mohawk rivers flow through eastern and southern New York. The Hudson rises in the Adirondack Mountains of northern New York. Near its mouth, the Hudson forms the boundary between the states of New York and New Jersey.

From its source in northern Minnesota, the Mississippi River runs 2,348 miles (3,779 km) southward to the Gulf of Mexico. Tributaries of this river include the Ohio (and its feeder river, the Tennessee) and the Missouri. The Ohio provided a vital route for settlers moving westward in the nineteenth century. The entire Mississippi-Ohio system still forms a key transportation network for U.S. goods.

The drier western regions have few navigable rivers. Rising in the Rocky Mountains, the Colorado River meets the Gila River in Arizona before winding toward the Gulf of California, an arm of the Pacific Ocean. Along its course of 1,450 miles (2,330 km), the Colorado passes through the Grand Canyon, a huge, steep-walled gorge.

The Columbia River flows for 1,214 miles (1,954 km) from western Canada through the northwestern United States. In Idaho the waterway merges with its largest tributary, the Snake River, before emptying into the Pacific Ocean near Portland, Oregon.

The waters of **the upper Mississippi River at Bellevue, Iowa,** flow at a rate of about 2 to 5 miles (3 to 8 km) per hour.

Climate

The climate in the United States varies greatly by region, elevation, and season. Most of the country, however, lies in the temperate zone of the Northern Hemisphere. Moderate temperatures and precipitation are typical of this zone, although weather conditions can become extreme.

In the northeastern United States, summers are generally warm and winters are cold. Average temperatures are 75°F (24°C) throughout the summer months. During the winter, the northern states experience low temperatures. Madison, Wisconsin, for example, averages 14°F (–10°C) in January, the coldest month. Farther south, in Saint Louis, Missouri, winter temperatures reach an average of 40°F (4°C). In the Southeast, summers are generally hot and humid, with temperatures ranging anywhere from 75°F to 90°F (24°C to 32°C). Average winter readings vary from 45°F (7°C) in Atlanta, Georgia, to 75°F (24°C) in Key West, Florida, where the climate is tropical. Winters in the West are also mild. Average January temperatures range from 40°F (4°C) in Seattle, Washington, to more than 60°F (16°C) in Los Angeles, California.

Precipitation in the eastern half of the United States is highest along the Atlantic and Gulf coasts and also in the southern two-thirds of the interior. Every summer and fall, hurricanes threaten the Gulf and Atlantic coasts. During the winter, cold air masses from Canada carry snow to the northern states. Here the average annual precipitation is about 30 inches (76 centimeters), but heavy snowfalls can deposit 12 inches (30 cm) or more at a time. In general, the western Great Plains region is dry, averaging about 15 inches (38 cm) of precipitation each year.

Dangerous thunderstorms are common in Florida during the spring and summer months. In late afternoon, as heat rises from the ground, it meets cooler air blowing east from the Gulf of Mexico. Storms unleash high winds, torrential rain, and dangerous lightning. Florida has more than twice as many lightning strikes as any other state.

Flora and Fauna

Forests of evergreens and stands of hardwood trees—such as oak, hickory, and walnut—dominate the eastern and north central sections of the United States. Bald cypress, tupelo, and white cedar trees grow in the swamps of the Southeast. Fir trees, as well as redwoods and bristlecone pines, thrive in the West. Tough desert plants of the Intermountain Region include cacti, yuccas, sagebrush, and mesquite. In contrast, the tropical zones of Hawaii and southern Florida sustain royal and thatch palms, which typically grow in warm, wet climates. Evergreen forests of western Washington and Oregon thrive in the largest temperate rain forest in the world.

Animal species found throughout the nation include white-tailed deer, black bears, bobcats, beavers, coyotes, and snapping turtles. American bison, once nearly extinct, roam wildlife preserves on the Great Plains. Panthers and alligators inhabit the low-lying marshes of the Everglades, in southern Florida. The waters off the Pacific coast are home to whales, dolphins, seals, and sea lions, while manatees (sea cows) swim off the coast of Florida.

The bald eagle flies throughout the United States, with the largest number of bald eagles in Alaska. The California condor, the largest flying land bird in North America, lives in mountainous regions of the West. Canadian geese, ducks, loons, mallards, teals, and mergansers are common in lakes and rivers of the North. Coastal areas of the Southeast are home to egrets, cormorants, herons, pelicans, ibis, and cranes.

By 1905 overhunting had reduced the **bison** population to only 500 in the United States and Canada. By careful management of wild and domestic herds since that time, North America has become home to more than 350,000 bison.

Natural Resources

The United States has a wide variety of natural resources, including minerals, trees, water, and soil. The country's most important resources are oil, natural gas, and coal, all vital resources for energy production. Alaska, California, Texas, Louisiana, Oklahoma, and the Gulf of Mexico have productive oil fields. Coal is abundant in the Appalachian Mountains and Wyoming. Mines in Michigan and northern Minnesota produce taconite. The iron and steel industries depend on this dense ore, although the vast surface mines leave the land stripped of all trees and vegetation.

Mines in the United States also produce copper, lead, tin, mercury, antimony, tungsten, nickel, silver, and zinc. Uranium mines supply a material once used in glass and chemical dyes but is more commonly used as a fuel in nuclear reactors. Gold mines have been producing since the nineteenth century in the Black Hills region of western South Dakota and in the deserts of Nevada.

Forests, covering about one-third of the United States, supply raw material for newsprint, building materials, turpentine, and other wood products. Hardwood trees (primarily oak) of the Appalachians provide wood for the furniture industry. Softwoods, such as Douglas fir, are used mainly as lumber and make up 80 percent of the trees felled in the United States.

Environmental Issues

Urban growth brings serious pollution of air, water, and land in the United States. Choking traffic in the major cities leads to smog, a haze of exhaust that often hangs low in the sky. Industrial waste runs into lakes and waterways that provide drinking water. Forestry and mining in the western states harm or destroy the natural environment.

The United States is also facing the issue of global warming. World temperatures have been on the rise for many years. Many scientists believe this trend is due to the burning of fossil fuels, such as coal and oil. If unchecked, global warming could bring permanent change to the earth's climate, with serious economic and social consequences.

In Gary and East Chicago, Indiana, **industrial emissions pollute** the air and the water.

Many nations have signed the Kyoto Treaty and agreed to limit the release of carbon dioxide and other "greenhouse gases" by their industries. However, the U.S. government believes the treaty could damage the U.S. economy. For that reason, the United States Senate has not signed the treaty.

Perhaps the most important environmental challenge is the nation's urban sprawl. The country's land and water resources are under pressure from the building of homes, office parks, shopping malls, and roads. This activity endangers many species of birds, fish, and animals that live close to populated areas.

> Information about the geography, wildlife, environmental issues, and major cities of the United States is plentiful on the Internet. Go to www.vgsbooks.com for links.

Major Cities

The United States is a largely urban nation, with 75 percent of the population living in cities and towns. The largest cities are New York, Los Angeles, and Chicago. Most U.S. cities sprawl across large metropolitan areas. In many places, suburbs include an even greater population than do the city limits. The Los Angeles metropolitan area, for example, holds three times as many people as the city itself. New York City has satellite towns in New Jersey, New York State, and Connecticut.

NEW YORK CITY New York City (population 7.3 million) is a world center of business and culture. It lies at the southeastern tip of New York State along the Hudson River. The city dates to 1624, when the Dutch settled on present-day Manhattan Island.

In 1825 the opening of the Erie Canal in upstate New York linked the city to the Great Lakes. This new market for New York City's industrial goods helped its manufacturing sector to expand. As a result, the city's population grew rapidly throughout the nineteenth century. In search of jobs and a new life, millions of immigrants have settled in New York, giving the city a greatly varied ethnic and cultural life.

Visitors are attracted to New York's world-famous theaters, museums, and monuments. The banks and stock exchanges of lower Manhattan make New York an international financial center. At the United Nations headquarters building, diplomats from around the world try to resolve international conflicts.

LOS ANGELES Sprawling across a desert basin in Southern California, Los Angeles (city population 4 million) is the second-largest city of the United States. The first known settlement on the site was a Shoshone Indian village. By the late eighteenth century, Spaniards had begun to settle in the area. Many of the city's modern inhabitants have their family origins in Mexico and other nations of Latin America.

The city's population soared in the late nineteenth century, when trains brought thousands of settlers from the eastern United States. The basin's warm and dry climate also drew filmmakers in the early twentieth century. Los Angeles has since become a world-renowned movie capital.

Los Angeles is the industrial and financial hub of the western United States. The manufacturing of aircraft and aerospace equipment, banking, the film industry, and tourism generate many of the

The Hollywood Walk of Fame in Los Angeles, California, honors U.S. entertainers. More than 2,500 pink terrazo stars were set into the sidewalk along a section of Hollywood Boulevard and Vine Street in 1960. Jerry Lewis, comedian and philanthropist, has a star *(bottom)*. In 2007 Matt Damon, Barbara Walters, and Sean (Diddy) Combs were among the celebrities to get stars.

city's jobs. The Port of Los Angeles, connected to the rest of the city by a narrow strip of land, is one of the world's busiest artificial harbors.

CHICAGO Chicago (city population 2.9 million) is in northeastern Illinois on the southwestern shore of Lake Michigan. Since the late nineteenth century, it has been a leading transportation hub. In 1959, when the Saint Lawrence Seaway opened up an all-water route from the Great Lakes to the Atlantic Ocean, Chicago also became a major seaport. The Chicago River links the city by canal to the Mississippi River.

With its port, railroads, and trucking firms, Chicago handles more freight than any other U.S. city. Chicago is also among the world's top industrial centers. Its factories make metals, foodstuffs, and many other products. In the bustling financial district, exchanges allow businesses to trade oil, gold, wheat, and other commodities.

WASHINGTON, D.C. The nation's capital since 1800, Washington, District of Columbia (city population 582,000, metro 5.8 million), is named after President George Washington. A French architect, Pierre Charles L'Enfant, laid out the city along the Potomac River between Maryland and Virginia.

As the headquarters of the national government, the District exists independently of any state. The city's buildings and memorials—including the White House, the U.S. Capitol, the Washington Monument, and the Lincoln Memorial—make Washington, D.C., a major tourist attraction. The U.S. government employs most of the area's workforce in service and administrative jobs.

HISTORY AND GOVERNMENT

About twenty thousand years ago, nomadic peoples began crossing a land bridge between northeastern Asia and present-day Alaska. These Paleo-Indians—the ancestors of modern Native Americans—migrated to the south and east. They hunted wild game to survive and gradually spread throughout North America.

By 300 B.C., Native Americans were farming in the southern Intermountain Region. They built permanent villages, some of which grew quite large. By the tenth century, the Hopewell and the Mississippian cultures had developed in the Mississippi River valley. These people raised huge earthen mounds for burying their dead.

The culture of the Mound Builders eventually disappeared. By the fifteenth century, however, about 1.5 million Native Americans, nomadic as well as settled, were living across the continent. Some traded extensively, using the rivers and lakes as their principal transportation routes. Depending partly on what their environment offered, they farmed, hunted, fished, or gathered food.

web enhanced @ www.vgsbooks.com

Early European Explorations

In 1492 the Italian explorer Christopher Columbus set out from a port in Spain. With three small vessels, Columbus was searching for a route to the East Indies. Instead of reaching the Indies, however, his small fleet landed in the Bahamas, an island group lying southeast of Florida.

Columbus returned to explore the Caribbean Sea three times. His voyages opened an unknown New World for Europe. Seafarers from Spain, France, and England sailed to North America. They converted many of the Native Americans, whom they knew as Indians, to Christianity.

The Italian explorer John Cabot, who sailed for the king of England, explored the Atlantic coast as early as 1497. Cabot claimed the shores and bays of northeastern North America for England. But the English monarchs waited a century before sending colonists to build settlements in the New World.

The Spaniards were the first Europeans to explore the North American interior. Juan Ponce de Leon landed in Florida in 1513. In 1539 Hernando de Soto searched for gold from Florida to the Mississippi River. During the 1540s, Francisco Vasquez de Coronado ventured from Mexico to the Great Plains.

Colonization

The English and the Spanish sent colonists to the North American wilderness. In 1565 the Spaniard Pedro Menéndez de Avilés established Saint Augustine, Florida. This was the first permanent European town in the United States. In 1585 the English founded a colony at Roanoke Island. This small island lies near the Outer Banks of North Carolina. In 1607 English settlers founded Jamestown, Virginia. Many of the Jamestown settlers died of starvation, disease, and attacks by Indians.

Religious sects seeking freedom of worship were also arriving. In 1620 Pilgrims from England established Plymouth. Shortly afterward, Puritans founded the colonies of Rhode Island, Connecticut, and Massachusetts Bay. Plymouth and Massachusetts Bay later became the colony of Massachusetts.

The Netherlands gained its foothold in North America in the early seventeenth century. The Dutch hired the Englishman Henry Hudson to explore the valley of a broad river, later named the Hudson River. His discoveries convinced the Dutch to organize the colony of New Netherland in 1624. This territory stretched from Cape Cod (in Massachusetts) to Delaware Bay (at the southern limit of New Jersey).

In later decades, French explorers pushed westward through the Great Lakes region and toward the Mississippi River. René-Robert Cavelier, Sieur de La Salle followed the river southward to its mouth at the Gulf of Mexico. In 1682 he claimed the entire Mississippi River region for France and named it Louisiana.

By the early eighteenth century, England had joined the United

NEW GIRL IN A NEW WORLD

On August 18, 1587, the English colonist Eleanor Dare gave birth to a baby girl at Roanoke, a settlement in present-day North Carolina. The girl, Virginia Dare, disappeared with her parents and the other Roanoke settlers in the next year. Only one clue to their fate remained behind: the word Croatoan–a reference to friendly Native Americans–carved into a post. Many historians believe the Roanoke colonists moved into nearby Native American villages. In later years, many of the Croatoan people were using English names and practicing Christianity. Whatever her fate, Virginia Dare remains the first child of European parents born in the New World.

Kingdom of Great Britain. By 1732 the British realm included thirteen colonies along the Atlantic coast. As the colonists pushed westward, they forced many surviving Native American groups off their lands. This caused violent conflicts on the western frontiers. To protect themselves and to claim new land, many of the colonies recruited young men into temporary militias.

By the mid-eighteenth century, the white population of British America had reached nearly 2 million. The importation of black slaves from Africa added about 500,000 inhabitants. In some colonies, the slaves outnumbered their owners. The planters used slaves to work fields of tobacco, cotton, and rice.

Meanwhile, British colonists began to venture farther west, into the territory of the French traders. Clashes erupted between colonists and the French, who allied with the Algonquin and Huron Indians. One of these conflicts triggered the French and Indian War (1754–1763). British troops and colonial militias allied with the Iroquois people and fought against the French. George Washington, a planter and surveyor from Virginia, commanded one of the militias.

To limit Britain's power, Spain and many Native American nations also allied with the French. But France lost the war and most of its claims in North America. Most French colonial territory went to Britain. France also ceded (gave up) the Louisiana Territory to Spain.

▶ Winning Independence

The end of the French and Indian War did not bring peace to North America. To protect the fur trade and fight the Native Americans, Britain's King George III sent troops to the thirteen colonies. To pay for the soldiers' food, clothing, and salaries, the king heavily taxed the colonies. The taxes met fierce resistance from colonists.

Many of the colonists in Massachusetts and elsewhere favored full independence. The British reacted by blockading Boston's harbor in 1774. The blockade prevented colonial merchants from exporting their goods.

In response, colonial leaders gathered at the first Continental Congress in Philadelphia, Pennsylvania. The king ignored the Congress's plea to change his policies. The colonies then refused to buy goods from Britain. After unsuccessfully urging Britain to withdraw its troops, the Continental Congress advised the people of Massachusetts to prepare for war.

The first clash of the American Revolution (1775–1783) took place in Massachusetts on April 19, 1775. Colonial and British soldiers skirmished at Lexington and Concord. The lightly armed colonists fought effectively against the slower British infantry. But many colonists saw an all-out war for independence as hopeless. The British maintained one of the world's strongest armies as well as a powerful navy. In addition, some colonists remained loyal to the British king. Others—including John Adams, George Washington, and Thomas Paine—supported rebellion. In 1776 Paine published *Common Sense*, a pamphlet that inspired thousands to oppose British rule.

As public support for the rebellion increased, the Continental Congress raised an army and asked George Washington to lead it. On July 4, 1776, the Congress passed the Declaration of Independence. This document stated that the British had failed to protect the basic rights and freedoms of the colonists. The declaration marked the colonies' official break from British rule.

Victory still seemed unlikely to many. Washington's army struggled with a lack of supplies and training. British forces defeated the colonists in Boston, New York, and Philadelphia. But the tide turned with the colonists' victory at Saratoga, New York, in 1777. In 1781 Washington's army stormed Yorktown, Virginia, and defeated its British garrison.

In 1783 the British signed the Treaty of Paris. The British recognized the former thirteen colonies as the independent United States of America. The new nation took possession of all British territory from the Atlantic coast westward to the Mississippi River.

The War of 1812

In 1787 leaders from the former colonies, now called states, met in Philadelphia to draw up the U.S. Constitution. Each state had to ratify (approve) the Constitution to be admitted into the United States of America.

George Washington (sitting behind desk), first president of the United States, presides over the signing of the U.S. Constitution in 1789. To learn more about the history of the United States from colonial to modern times, go to www.vgsbooks.com for links.

In the early nineteenth century, the new country expanded westward to the Mississippi River. In 1801, during the Napoleonic Wars in Europe, France regained control of the Louisiana Territory. Two years later, the French leader Napoleon Bonaparte sold it to the United States. This Louisiana Purchase doubled the size of the United States. The country's western boundary moved from the Mississippi River almost to the Rocky Mountains.

Meanwhile, the United States was expanding its commercial links to Europe. The Napoleonic Wars, however, sparked conflict with Britain. The British were kidnapping U.S. sailors and forcing them to serve in the British navy. And the British government was providing Native American groups with weapons to use against western settlers.

The U.S. Congress called for war against Britain in 1812. The two nations fought battles in the Atlantic Ocean and in the Great Lakes area. The British even attacked Washington, D.C., the U.S. capital. During the occupation of the capital, the British burned the White House and other federal buildings. But Britain could not sustain an effective army in distant North America. In 1814 the two countries signed a peace treaty.

Conflict on the Frontiers

Following the War of 1812, traders, soldiers, and settlers began moving west of the Appalachians. To encourage settlement, the U.S. government built forts and supply depots. From these bases, soldiers could attack Native Americans who were resisting the invasion of their land. To promote more westward movement, the U.S. government established territories on the frontier.

The demand for farmland prompted the U.S. government to buy or take land from Native Americans who lived in the territories. In the 1830s, the government forced the Creek, Chickasaw, Cherokee, Seminole, and Choctaw peoples to move to a reservation known as Indian Territory (covering Oklahoma). Hundreds of Native Americans died along the route, known as the Trail of Tears.

Steamboats and railroads moved people and goods to the western territories and states. The Erie Canal in upstate New York linked the Atlantic states with the Great Lakes region. The Great Lakes became an important manufacturing center.

Farther west, Americans were moving to territories claimed by Mexico. Some of these newcomers drew up their own laws in defiance of the Mexican government. These actions led to the Mexican-American War (1846–1848), which the United States won. The Treaty of Guadalupe Hidalgo ended the conflict in 1848. This agreement brought Mexican territories in Texas, New Mexico, Arizona, Colorado, Utah, and California into the United States.

In 1848 miners found gold in California. The discovery drew thousands of people to the Pacific coast. By 1850 white settlers made up nearly 70 percent of California's population. They greatly outnumbered Native Americans as well as Mexicans, whose roots in the area went back to the sixteenth century.

Civil War and Reconstruction

The economy of the industrial North was linked to the agricultural economy of the southern states. Northern cloth mills, for example, depended on the cotton grown on large southern plantations that used slave labor. Slavery, however, had been outlawed in the North. Nevertheless, in the Dred Scott decision of 1854, the U.S. Supreme Court declared that escaped slaves remained the property of their owners.

The southern states still allowed slavery. Southern plantation owners reasoned that they could not produce cotton at a profit without slaves. Some northerners argued that slavery should be abolished (made illegal) throughout the United States. This issue led to conflict between abolitionist states and slave-owning states. The Kansas Territory became the scene of violent skirmishes. Those who believed slavery should be legal in Kansas fought abolitionists who wanted to ban it in the new territory.

Abraham Lincoln, a northerner from Illinois, won the presidency in November 1860. Lincoln wanted to prohibit slavery in new territories. Southerners saw this as a threat to their rights and their livelihood. To protest, the southern state of South Carolina seceded (left) the United States in December 1860.

By 1861 a total of eleven southern states had followed South Carolina's example. They formed the Confederate States of America. The Confederacy established a capital in Richmond, Virginia, and elected Jefferson Davis as president.

Lincoln saw these actions as a dire threat to the future of the United States. He sent seventy-five thousand soldiers to strengthen government forts in the South. In the spring of 1861, the Civil War (1861–1865) broke out. Union soldiers from the North fought the Confederate forces of the South. The two huge armies clashed in dozens of bloody battles, including Bull Run, Antietam, Gettysburg, and Shiloh.

To end the war, Lincoln threatened to use his executive authority to free the slaves in the South. The Confederacy refused to surrender. On January 1, 1863, Lincoln's Emancipation Proclamation decreed an end to slavery in the rebellious states. The South did not recognize the emancipation. But many slaves were escaping to the North, using a network of secret routes and safe houses called the Underground Railroad. Thousands of former slaves joined the Union army.

Henry Brown escaped from slavery in Virginia by mailing himself in a small box to the Pennsylvania Abolitionist Society in Philadelphia. Slaves and the people who helped them on the Underground Railroad took great risks.

Without slave labor to raise crops for export, the South ran out of money and vital supplies. By 1864—after three years of stalemate—the North had gained the upper hand. Confederate leaders became convinced that continuing the war would be futile. On April 9, 1865, Union general Ulysses S. Grant accepted the surrender of Confederate general Robert E. Lee.

From 1865 to 1877, a period known as Reconstruction, the U.S. government rebuilt the South. To be readmitted to the Union, states that had seceded had to ratify the Fourteenth Amendment to the Constitution. The amendment (change) stated that all people born in the United States, including former slaves, were U.S. citizens. Native Americans, however, still did not have citizenship.

Most white southerners resented the control of their states by the U.S. government. As they regained power, they turned on the African American population. Local officials, for instance, enacted laws that made it difficult for African American men to vote or to receive an education. Secret radical groups, such as the Ku Klux Klan, terrorized African Americans with beatings and lynchings (executions outside of the law).

Settling the Frontier

During and after the Civil War, the U.S. government offered homesteads (free land) to settlers in the western territories. Land-hungry settlers rushed to the Great Plains and the mountains of the western United States. A small army of workers built a Transcontinental Railroad through the Rocky Mountains. The railway encouraged settlers to move across the mountains to California and the Pacific Northwest. Gold miners traveled as far as Alaska, which the United States bought from Russia in 1867.

Meanwhile, conflict between settlers and Native Americans worsened. The government signed treaties with the Plains people to separate them from the settlers. The U.S. Army built a string of forts along the rivers and trails. Cavalry soldiers often clashed with Native Americans, who raided wagon trains and settlements. Hunting destroyed the massive bison herds that Native Americans depended on for food, clothing, and shelter.

By 1890 U.S. troops had moved most of the remaining Native Americans onto reservations. These actions opened more western lands to settlement. Miners worked claims in the Rocky Mountains. Small towns grew along wagon trails and railroad lines in the Great Plains. Farmers, ranchers, and cowboys brought crops, cattle, and sheep to the towns to be shipped to eastern markets.

Industrialization

The United States' wealth of natural resources and a growing transportation network fueled economic growth. Eastern factories supplied iron and steel for the railways, machinery, and new construction. Textile mills provided the raw material for clothing factories. The discovery of oil in Pennsylvania gave birth to a petroleum industry.

Factories employed a large and growing labor force. Jobs opportunities in the growing economy attracted a wave of immigrant workers. Between 1890 and 1914, about 16 million immigrants—mostly from Russia, Poland, Italy, Greece, Slovakia, and Bohemia—entered the United States looking for work.

Conditions in the cities were grim for many of the new arrivals. In the factories, many adult and child laborers worked long days for low wages. Families lived in crowded and unhealthy apartments. To demand better wages and working conditions, some industrial workers started unions. Employers strongly opposed this trend. The conflict led to frequent labor strikes and violence in the streets.

By the end of the nineteenth century, U.S. business leaders had created several monopolies. A monopoly company, such as Standard Oil, dominated a single industry. The largest monopolies controlled the railroad, steel, and petroleum industries. Monopolies could charge customers high prices for goods or services. To avoid regulation by the government, many monopolies bribed local, state, and national legislators.

Rapid industrialization and population growth were bringing other economic and social problems. Progressive reformers set out to address these issues. These reformers passed laws to regulate monopolies, establish building codes, allow unions to form, and enforce child labor laws.

Foreign Wars and Depression

Throughout these decades, the United States had largely stayed out of international affairs. Some U.S. leaders felt the country should use its power and wealth to acquire foreign territories. Others wanted to avoid foreign conflicts. Wars and treaty negotiations in the late nineteenth century ended U.S. isolation.

In 1898 an explosion destroyed the battleship USS *Maine* in Havana, Cuba, then a colony of Spain. Newspapers in the United States accused Spain of this act. The accusations pushed the two nations into war. The United States won the Spanish-American War (1898) and seized the Spanish colonies of Puerto Rico, Guam, the Philippine Islands, and Cuba (which won its independence in 1902). In 1898 the United States also made the Hawaiian Islands a U.S. territory.

At the start of World War I (1914–1918), the United States remained neutral in a conflict that pitted Germany against Britain and France. But in 1917, German submarines attacked several U.S. merchant ships. The United States entered the war on the side of France and Britain. More than two million U.S. troops sailed overseas to help defeat Germany.

After the war, the United States enjoyed a decade of prosperity. Expanding U.S. industries produced cars, refrigerators, and washing machines. American society went through important changes as well. With the Eighteenth Amendment to the Constitution, the sale and possession of alcohol became illegal. In 1920 women gained the right to vote with the passage of the Nineteenth Amendment.

People from farms and small towns migrated to urban areas. For the first time, a majority of the country's population lived in cities. But the economic boom ended in 1929, with the crash of the New York stock market. Investors lost money, factories closed, and jobs disappeared.

One of the worst urban disasters in U.S. history took place in Boston, in 1919. A molasses tank at the Purity Distilling Company burst, spilling 2 million gallons (7.6 million liters) of the sticky stuff into the streets. The gigantic wave reached a height of 15 feet (4.5 m) and derailed a train on the nearby Boston Elevated Railway. It then moved through the North End of the city at 35 miles (56 km) per hour, killing 21 people and injuring 150.

The stock market crash began the Great Depression (1929–1942). In the cities, jobless people begged on the streets. In the Great Plains, droughts and strong winds killed crops and blew away fertile topsoil.

To combat the Depression, the administration of President Franklin Roosevelt drew up the New Deal in 1933. This series of programs offered food, money, and jobs to millions of unemployed people. The New Deal provided an economic safety net for those facing hunger and homelessness.

In the late 1930s, war again threatened many parts of Europe. U.S. factories made weapons and other heavy goods. The U.S. military added ships, tanks, and other equipment to its arsenal. The upturn in production prepared the nation for World War II (1939–1945).

The war broke out in Europe in September 1939, when Germany invaded Poland. In 1941 Germany attacked the Soviet Union, a federation of fifteen republics, including Russia. The Allies (including Canada, Britain, France, China, and the Soviet Union) opposed the Axis powers of Germany, Italy, and Japan.

Most Americans wanted to stay out of the war. On December 7, 1941, however, the Japanese attacked Pearl Harbor, a U.S. naval base in the Hawaiian Islands. The next day, the United States declared war on Japan. Germany and Italy soon joined Japan's effort to defeat the United States.

The U.S. military took part in many sea and land battles. Ships ferried U.S. supplies to Asia, Africa, and Europe. The United States invaded Axis-occupied North Africa, then Italy. The Allies staged a massive invasion of German-occupied France in 1944. Italy withdrew from the war, and Germany surrendered in May 1945. The United States destroyed Hiroshima and Nagasaki, Japan, with deadly atomic bombs in August 1945. Soon afterward, Japan surrendered.

On December 7, 1941, **Japanese bombs poured down on Pearl Harbor** on the Hawaiian island of Oahu. Twenty-one ships sank or were destroyed, and more than 2,400 Americans died. The attack prompted the United States to enter the war against the Axis powers.

The Cold War

After World War II ended, the United States and the Soviet Union emerged as the world's two superpowers. The Soviet Union had occupied nations in Eastern Europe and had established Communist governments. (Under Communism, one political party controls the economy, education, government, and the media.) The United States, favoring free markets and private ownership, strived to stop the spread of Communism to other countries.

To strengthen its influence, the United States set up the North Atlantic Treaty Organization (NATO). This military alliance included several Western European nations. In response, the Soviet Union and its allies signed a similar treaty called the Warsaw Pact.

As Europe and Japan rebuilt, the United States opposed the Soviet Union in a global Cold War (1945–1991). Both sides built arsenals of nuclear arms and stationed military forces in Europe. The United States intervened to prevent Communist takeovers in several countries.

This policy led the United States into the Korean War (1950–1953) and then the Vietnam War (1957–1975). Once a French colony, Vietnam was divided into a Communist north and a U.S.-allied south. Communist guerrillas (rebels) in the South sought to overthrow the government there and unify the country. President John F. Kennedy began sending advisers to Vietnam. In 1963 he was assassinated in Dallas, Texas. Vice President Lyndon Johnson became president and soon ordered more troops to Vietnam. Beginning in 1965, U.S. ground troops battled these guerrillas and the North Vietnamese army.

Meanwhile, the United States was experiencing social turmoil. Led by activists such as Dr. Martin Luther King Jr., African Americans were protesting racial segregation. The policy of segregation separated white and minority populations in public places. It also barred minorities from equal opportunities in jobs, education, and housing.

The protests eventually brought change. In 1964 Congress passed the Civil Rights Act. This law made it illegal to discriminate against blacks and other minorities. It did not, however, end racial violence in U.S. cities. In 1968 an assassin shot and killed King in Memphis, Tennessee. Even while domestic and foreign conflict plagued the country, the United States managed a stunning technological breakthrough, by landing astronauts on the moon in 1969.

The civil rights movement inspired a drive for equality among women, Native Americans, and Latinos—people of Latin American ancestry. The union leader Cesar Chavez, a Mexican American, organized farmworkers in California. In 1973 hundreds of Native Americans occupied the site of Wounded Knee, where the last battle between the U.S. cavalry and the Sioux had taken place in 1890.

Meanwhile, many Americans were protesting U.S. involvement in Vietnam. The war remained a stalemate. In time, a majority of people were demanding that the United States pull out of the conflict. By 1973 President Richard Nixon had withdrawn all U.S. troops from Vietnam. Nixon then faced a political scandal known as Watergate. The scandal involved illegal actions taken by Nixon and his staff during the 1972 presidential race. In 1974 the scandal forced Nixon to resign, a decision no previous president had ever made.

The United States was not the only superpower with problems. In the late 1980s, Warsaw Pact governments faced massive public protests. These protests brought down the Communist governments in Eastern Europe. In 1991 the Soviet Union broke up into fifteen independent republics. The Soviet Communist Party fell from power. This left the United States as the world's only superpower.

The fall of the United States' Cold War rival did not end its involvement in foreign conflicts. In 1990 the Middle East nation of Iraq invaded Kuwait, an oil-rich U.S. ally on the Persian Gulf. The United States formed a coalition of military allies and attacked Iraqi forces in 1991. The first Gulf War quickly liberated Kuwait.

On the African continent, U.S. troops brought humanitarian relief to war-torn Somalia. The fighting drew in U.S. troops, who suffered casualties and soon withdrew. In 1993 the United States staged air raids over Serbia, part of the former nation of Yugoslavia. U.S. military planes also dropped food and medical supplies to Serbia's rival, Bosnia-Herzegovina. U.S. involvement eventually led to a truce in the fighting.

A War on Terrorism

The United States was also subject to terrorist attacks. In 1993 a group of terrorists set off a large bomb underneath the World Trade Center in New York City. In 1995 a truck bomb destroyed a U.S. government building and killed more than one hundred people in downtown Oklahoma City, Oklahoma. U.S. citizens opposed in principle to the U.S. government carried out the attack.

President Bill Clinton, who was elected in 1992 and reelected in 1996, went through a troubling scandal during his second term. Under oath, he was caught lying about a sexual affair. The House of Representatives voted to impeach the president. A vote against him in the Senate would have ended his presidency. He survived the Senate vote, however, by a narrow margin.

The presidential election of 2000 caused another dispute. Vice President Al Gore, the Democrat candidate, won a majority of the vote. His opponent, George W. Bush, however, won a victory in the Electoral College, which decides the election outcome. (Each state has the same number of electoral votes as it has members in the House of Representatives and the Senate.) Bush's margin of victory in Florida was close, and Gore demanded a recount. The dispute went to the Supreme Court, where the nine justices voted narrowly to stop the recount.

On September 11, 2001, the United States was the target of another devastating terrorist attack. Hijackers captured four passenger planes and flew three of them into large public buildings. The attacks caused more than three thousand deaths. The U.S. government accused al-Qaeda, a terrorist network operating from the central Asian nation of Afghanistan, of carrying out the attacks.

President Bush declared a War on Terrorism. Bush announced that he would consider any country harboring terrorists an enemy of the United States. That fall the United States attacked the Taliban government of Afghanistan. U.S. forces also attacked al-Qaeda camps and overthrew the Taliban.

Soon afterward, the United States gathered another invasion force in the Persian Gulf. Claiming that Iraq still held dangerous nuclear and chemical weapons, Bush ordered an attack on the Iraqi regime. In April 2003, U.S. forces defeated armies loyal to Saddam Hussein, the Iraqi leader, and drove him from power.

The United States set up elections and a representative government in Iraq. Bush said that the goal was to provide a model of democracy for the Middle East. But the U.S. occupation of Afghanistan and Iraq sparked opposition and armed rebellion in both countries. The indecisive war in Iraq was costing thousands of U.S. dead and wounded. The conflict also lost public support in the United States.

The Pentagon in Washington, DC, was a terrorist target on September 11, 2001.
The day after the attack, George W. Bush *(center)* greeted firefighters at the site. He had been the U.S. president for less than one year at the time.

Hurricane Katrina flooded New Orleans, Louisiana, in August 2005. Large parts of the city remained unrepaired and uninhabitable for years. Go to www.vgsbooks.com for links to the latest news about the United States.

A natural disaster struck in the summer of 2005, when Hurricane Katrina hit the Gulf of Mexico coast. Heavy rains and high winds broke several levees (water barriers) in the city of New Orleans. Severe flooding resulted. Thousands of people were stranded on rooftops and highway bridges. The government's slow rescue operations inspired widespread criticism.

Opposition to the war in Iraq turned many voters against President Bush. In the fall of 2006, members of the Democratic Party—Bush's opponents—won majority status in Congress. Democrats controlled the Senate as well as the House of Representatives. In 2007 Congress demanded a timetable for withdrawal of U.S. forces. President Bush opposed such a timetable and promised to veto any measure that contained one.

The issue of immigration emerged as a vital issue in the first years of the twenty-first century. Each year thousands of immigrants illegally cross the U.S-Mexican border to seek work in the United States. The crossings sparked protest against lax border controls. At the same time, Hispanic Americans protested against prosecution of illegal immigrants. Immigration laws, as well as policies regarding Iraq and the environment, will be at the forefront of the presidential election in 2008.

⊙ Government

The Constitution of the United States sets forth the powers of the national and state governments. The Constitution also provides for three U.S. branches of government—executive, legislative, and judicial. These three branches work together to run the country. This separation of powers gives each branch some independence and balances the U.S. government.

The executive branch includes the president and vice president. The president is the chief executive officer and chief of state. The president's main responsibilities include enforcing federal laws, appointing U.S. officials, commanding the armed forces, and conducting foreign affairs. The presidential elections take place every four years.

The U.S. Congress is the legislative branch of government. This branch consists of the Senate and the House of Representatives. Congress is responsible for making, repealing, and amending federal laws. The Senate approves federal appointments and international treaties. It has one hundred members—two from each state—who serve six-year terms. The number of representatives a state sends to the House is determined by the state's population.

The judicial branch is made up of the U.S. Supreme Court, ninety-five federal district courts, and twelve federal courts of appeal. With Senate approval, the president appoints the nine judges of the Supreme Court, who serve for life or until they choose to retire. The Supreme Court, the highest court in the nation, hears important cases involving constitutional principles.

Voters in the states elect governors and legislators. Mayors and city councils administer the cities. County governments handle planning, sheriff's departments, and basic services.

Many important legal decisions have been made in the **Supreme Court building** in Washington, D.C. Each year the Supreme Court justices begin work on the first Monday in October and finish in June or July.

THE PEOPLE

In the early twenty-first century, the U.S. population reached 300 million. Every year the nation averages 14 births, 8 deaths, and 3 new immigrants per 1,000 people. This gives the United States a population growth rate of 0.6 percent every year. By 2025 the country will be home to about 350 million people.

The nation's average population density—80 people per square mile (31 people per sq. km)—does not reflect an even distribution of people. Sections of the Northeast and the Pacific coast are heavily populated. New Jersey has the highest population density in the country, at 1,134 people per square mile (438 people per sq. km). The central United States, the mountainous regions, Alaska, and Hawaii hold fewer people. Alaska is the most sparsely populated and home to about 1 person per square mile (0.4 person per sq. km).

The United States has been an urban nation since the 1920s, when a majority of people began living in cities. Since then many more families have moved away from rural small towns. As large companies bought family farms, the trend continued. Population loss has hit hard in the rural Midwest, where some settlements have become ghost towns.

In the late twentieth century, population trends in the United States made an important shift. As heavy industry slowed in the Midwest and Northeast, people moved away. Population increased in southern and western states. Older cities, such as Cleveland, Buffalo, and Detroit lost population. Phoenix, Atlanta, Miami, and other southern cities grew much larger. High-tech industries drew people to the Pacific coast. In addition, the arrival of Latin American immigrants boosted population in California, Florida, and Texas.

Ethnic Groups

Most newcomers to the American colonies came from England, Germany, and the Netherlands. By the nineteenth century, French, Irish, and Scandinavian peoples were crossing the Atlantic Ocean. The immigrants were searching for political freedom and economic opportunity. Immigrants from nations in eastern Europe and southern Europe began arriving in the late nineteenth century. As a result, about three-fourths of the U.S. population has European ancestry.

In colonial times, the slave trade brought captive Africans to North America. Their descendants account for about 12 percent of the population. African Americans moved north after the Civil War, which ended slavery. They settled in large cities that offered well-paid jobs. More recently, black immigrants have arrived from the East African nations of Somalia and Ethiopia and from the Caribbean nations of Jamaica and Haiti. Many of these new arrivals hold unskilled jobs in factories and in service industries, such as restaurants and hotels. Often immigrants work as household maids, nannies, and delivery and taxi drivers.

Latinos—people from Latin America—make up 9 percent of the overall U.S. population. Most Latinos in the United States arrived from Mexico and Central America. They make up a large segment of

> The U.S. government estimates that the country will have 40 million foreign-born people by the year 2010. Most–nearly 10 million–will come from Mexico. Other important home countries, in order, will be China, the Philippines, India, Ireland, Cuba, and El Salvador–all with more than 1 million immigrants.

An employee of the National Resources Conservation Service in Okaloosa County, Florida, studies a field for potential problems. Many **Latinos work in science, engineering, and other technical jobs.**

the population in California, Arizona, New Mexico, and Texas. Many South American immigrants arrive in Miami, Florida. This city has become a melting pot of Latin nationalities, home to people from Cuba, Colombia, Peru, Venezuela, Argentina, and Brazil.

About 3 percent of the U.S. population has family origins in China, India, Vietnam, Laos, Cambodia, Japan, Korea, or the Philippines. The ancestry of many Asian American families dates to the mid-nineteenth century. At that time, laborers from eastern Asia came to work in western mines or on the railways. Recently, hundreds of thousands have emigrated from Asia to the United States.

The end of the Vietnam War in 1975 brought Vietnamese refugees to California and Texas. On the West Coast, Vietnamese business owners operate grocery stores, nail salons, restaurants, and video rental shops. In Texas Vietnamese fishers catch shrimp in the Gulf of Mexico. This community later spread to major cities in the Midwest and in the northeastern United States.

Only 1 percent of the population is Native American. The largest Native American nations are Cherokee, Navajo, Sioux, and Ojibwe. Many Native Americans live on reservations. These are semi-independent territories, mostly in the West. The reservations have long faced hard economic times. Jobs and industry are generally scarce, while residents struggle with health and social problems. But for some Native American nations, new tourist businesses, such as casinos, have brought rising income.

The United States has one of the world's most diverse populations. Many call it a melting pot: a place where different ethnic groups have adopted a common culture. Most people speak English, wear similar fashions, and enjoy the same types of recreation. On the other hand, many groups strive to maintain their cultural identities. They speak their own languages, organize traditional festivals, and attend their own religious services. As new immigrant groups arrive, the mix of cultures grows more complex.

▶ Health and Welfare

The United States has a large network of public and private hospitals and clinics. Some private companies pay a portion of their employees' health insurance. Medicare is an insurance program for the elderly. Medicaid provides medical benefits to some of the poor. In addition, many public health departments offer immunizations, laboratory tests, and other services to help prevent the spread of illnesses.

Heart disease is the leading cause of death in the United States. About 28 percent of deaths each year result from heart conditions. Cancer is another major health problem, causing about 22 percent of

TAKE A SICK DAY!

Mary Mallon was perhaps the most unpopular woman in U.S. history. She emigrated from Ireland in 1883 at the age of fourteen. She worked as a cook for wealthy families in New York and surrounding towns. She infected forty-seven people in these homes with typhoid fever, a highly infectious disease. She didn't believe she was to blame and even helped to care for the sick. By doing this, she spread the disease even further. She also refused to stop working, much to the dismay of local health officials. As a result, they forced "Typhoid Mary" to live in a hospital for twenty years until she died in 1938—of pneumonia.

all deaths. The country is also struggling to combat strokes, diabetes, and respiratory diseases (many caused by smoking). Alzheimer's disease, causing memory loss, affects about 4 million people over the age of sixty. Among the very young, autism is a growing problem. An autistic child has difficulty interacting with others or responding to the environment.

About 0.6 percent of the people between fifteen and forty-nine have HIV (human immunodeficiency virus). The rate of new infection held steady in the early twenty-first century at about forty thousand cases each year. The incidence is highest in the Northeast, in the South, and in California. Scientists generally believe this virus causes AIDS (acquired immunodeficiency syndrome). AIDS patients have weakened immune systems and suffer a wide

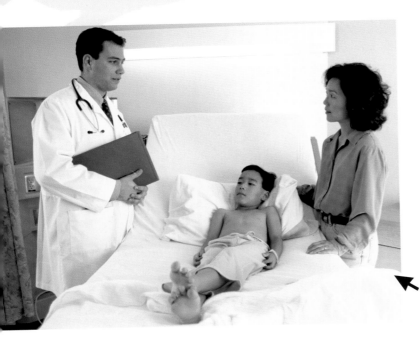

A hospital pediatrician (*left*) consults a worried mother. The high—and rising—cost of health insurance is a big issue in the United States.

range of serious illnesses. U.S. and state governments have launched campaigns to educate the public about AIDS prevention and testing.

The average life expectancy of people born in the United States is 78 years (75 for males and 80 for females). This is equal to or slightly lower than the figures for other developed countries. The nation's infant mortality rate—the number of babies that die before their first birthday—stands at 6.3 deaths out of every 1,000 live births. This figure is slightly higher than the rate in Canada. Infant mortality stems in part from a lack of proper medical care before birth.

U.S. citizens benefit from an extensive system of social welfare. Social Security is a pension plan that draws payments from workers and employers. Its benefits are available to retired persons, the disabled, and surviving members of a family that has lost its principle wage earner. Qualifying individuals can also draw unemployment benefits. Welfare payments can temporarily support needy families with children. A new law passed in 1996 limited these benefits to sixty months during a recipient's lifetime.

In the twenty-first century, the Social Security system is dealing with financial challenges. As the birthrate declines, the U.S. population is slowly growing older. The number of retirees is rising and drawing out more money. So, the system has become a subject of political debate. If contributions do not keep up with paid benefits, the system could face a crisis.

Learn more about U.S. ethnic groups, language issues, health, and education. Go to www.vgsbooks.com for links.

 ## Language

The U.S. government has never named an official national language. In early colonial days, European settlers spoke English, Dutch, French, or German. After the Revolutionary War, English emerged as the principal language of business, the legal system, government, and the media.

Historically, immigrants used their native tongues in their homes and ethnic neighborhoods. In public schools, however, instruction took place largely in English. Eventually, states and cities passed laws requiring the use of English. Knowledge of English became the route to jobs and better opportunity for new immigrants.

Spanish has become the second most common tongue in the United States. About 12 percent of the population uses it as a first or second language. Some people in cities with large Latino populations

At the **Navajo Elementary School in Navajo, New Mexico,** a Navajo teacher helps a young student with her schoolwork. They may speak and write Navajo as well as English in the classroom.

support the public use of Spanish as well as English. Others argue that the use of a single language helps to unify a nation. Some states have passed laws making English their state's official language.

Much of the Native American community is bilingual, with members knowing English and their original languages. The Nadene family of Native American languages, which includes Navajo, is the largest in the United States. Nadene languages survive in Arizona, New Mexico, California, and along the Pacific coast north to Alaska.

Education

State and local governments are in charge of public education. In most states, students attend elementary school for five or six years, middle school for three years, and high school for three or four years. About 85 percent of students attend public primary and secondary schools.

Public education is free through grade twelve and compulsory up to the age of sixteen to eighteen in most states. Most students attend classes five days a week, for six or seven hours a day. Public schools also offer sports and job training programs. In many school districts, summer vacation allows students a break of two to three months. In the past, the summer break allowed rural students to help with the harvest of crops. The tradition has continued even as the country has become largely urban.

Students pay tuition to church-run and other private schools. These schools can set their own curriculum and grading system. They also control classroom size, an important factor in the quality of schooling. Some families keep their children out of schools altogether. Instead of sending them to private or public schools, they teach their children in private homes. Each state has its own laws and guidelines regarding homeschoolers.

About 97 percent of the people living in the United States can read and write—an average number compared to other developed nations. By the law of most states, public school systems use the dominant language, English. Some schools also use Spanish, the language of many young immigrants.

About 75 percent of students graduate from high school after twelve years of education. The dropout rate in the United States is high for a developed nation. But more than half of the nation's high school graduates continue their education at institutions of higher learning. Public and private universities in the United States draw students from all over the world.

About 45 percent of the colleges and universities are public institutions. There are also many specialized colleges. Gallaudet University in Washington, D.C., welcomes deaf students. Howard and Grambling universities are the leading African American institutions. Many Indian reservations have small colleges serving local Native American students. The U.S. government runs military academies to train officers in the U.S. Army, Navy, and Air Force.

AMERICAN SIGN LANGUAGE

At a school for the hearing-impaired in Hartford, Connecticut, an entirely new language began in the early nineteenth century. This American Sign Language (ASL) has its own vocabulary, syntax, and grammar. Many of its hand signs came from a sign language used on the island of Martha's Vineyard, off the coast of Massachusetts. This island had many deaf residents, as one of its early founders passed on genetic hearing loss to his descendants. In the early twentieth century, as more outsiders moved to the island and American Sign Language grew in popularity, Martha's Vineyard Sign Language became extinct.

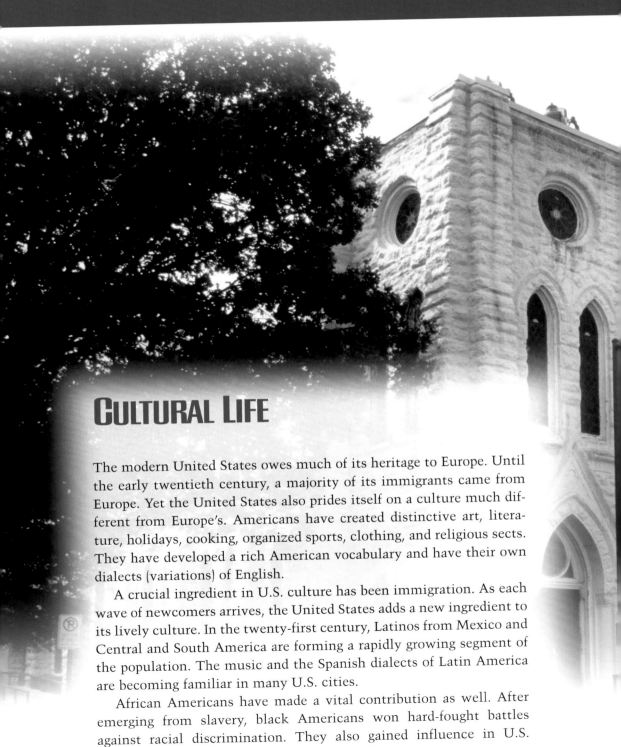

CULTURAL LIFE

The modern United States owes much of its heritage to Europe. Until the early twentieth century, a majority of its immigrants came from Europe. Yet the United States also prides itself on a culture much different from Europe's. Americans have created distinctive art, literature, holidays, cooking, organized sports, clothing, and religious sects. They have developed a rich American vocabulary and have their own dialects (variations) of English.

A crucial ingredient in U.S. culture has been immigration. As each wave of newcomers arrives, the United States adds a new ingredient to its lively culture. In the twenty-first century, Latinos from Mexico and Central and South America are forming a rapidly growing segment of the population. The music and the Spanish dialects of Latin America are becoming familiar in many U.S. cities.

African Americans have made a vital contribution as well. After emerging from slavery, black Americans won hard-fought battles against racial discrimination. They also gained influence in U.S.

culture, especially in music, writing, cooking, and organized sports. Immigrants and their descendants have taken up Native American art, music, and religious ceremony. The Native American outlook has inspired a movement to protect the environment and natural resources.

Religion

More than one thousand different religious groups exist in the United States. Some sects—including Seventh-day Adventists, the Church of Jesus Christ of Latter-day Saints (Mormons), Jehovah's Witnesses, and Christian Scientists—began in the United States. Other religions arrived with immigrants from Europe, Asia, and the Middle East.

About 75 percent of the nation's citizens are members of the Christian religion. Of these, about 25 percent have ties to the Roman Catholic Church. Catholics make up the largest single denomination in the United States. Protestants, whose sects originated in sixteenth-century Europe, make up the other 75 percent. The largest Protestant sects are Baptist, Methodist, and Lutheran. Several Anabaptist sects, including the Amish, hold to traditional ways in rural areas. The United States is also home to Eastern Orthodox believers. The Mormons date their Christian sect to the nineteenth century. Many live in Utah, a territory first settled by Mormon believers.

Jews and Muslims (followers of the Islamic faith) sustain large religious communities. The United States is also home to Hindus and Sikhs, from the Indian subcontinent of South Asia. Buddhists follow the teachings of the ancient Indian philosopher Siddhartha Gautama. Altogether, 10 percent of the population belongs to non-Christian faiths. About 15 percent of the population claims to be agnostic or atheist and have no connection to an organized church.

Literature

Native Americans have a long tradition of myth and sacred literature. Storytellers and singers passed down these tales to younger generations, shaping their beliefs and outlook on the world. Each nation had a unique creation myth, often describing a creator of the sky and the natural elements. In Native American literature, the elements of

Some **Jewish families such as this one fled to the United States** to escape Russian pograms (fierce anti-Jewish riots) in the late 1800s and early 1900s. Many immigrants have come to the United States to escape religious persecution in their homelands.

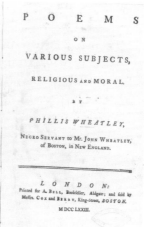

Poems by **Phillis Wheatley** were published as a book in 1773. This portrait of Wheatley at her writing desk appears opposite of the book's title page.

wind, air, fire, and water played an important role. The ghosts of the dead sometimes mingled among the living. Lesser spirits appeared in the form of sacred animals, such as the wolf or bear.

As Europeans settled the continent, a publishing industry emerged in Boston, Philadelphia, and New York. The short pamphlet and almanac were popular reading for the American colonists. Many were inspired to rebellion by the writings of Thomas Paine and Samuel Adams. Phillis Wheatley, who was captured in Africa and sold into slavery, wrote her first poem, *On Messrs. Hussey and Coffin*, at the age of twelve. Her book *Poems on Various Subjects, Religious and Moral* was published in 1773, the first published work of an African American woman.

The authors and poets of the United States forged new literary styles in the mid-nineteenth century. Edgar Allan Poe and Nathaniel Hawthorne developed the short story into a respected literary form. Louisa May Alcott wrote *Little Women* and other novels for young readers. Among the greatest poets of the era were Emily Dickinson, Ralph Waldo Emerson, Walt Whitman, and Henry Wadsworth Longfellow. Harriet Beecher Stowe's *Uncle Tom's Cabin* fueled a national debate on

A MYSTERIOUS DEATH

The writer Edgar Allan Poe penned the world's first detective story, *The Murders in the Rue Morgue*. In this tale, a skilled sleuth discovers the secrets to a murder. Poe's own death was also mysterious. He was found on a Baltimore street, drunk, unkempt, raving, and not wearing his own clothes. He died a few days later in a hospital. Historians believe that Poe may have been held captive, plied with drink, perhaps beaten, and then forced to vote in an election—repeatedly—by thugs working for a local politician. This was a fairly common occurrence then in city elections.

slavery. In the late nineteenth century, Mark Twain used realistic and comical dialects in portraying his adventurous characters, such as *The Adventures of Tom Sawyer* and *The Adventures of Huckleberry Finn*.

Mark Twain

Industrialization, World War I, and the Great Depression turned some writers to the social problems facing the country. Upton Sinclair and John Steinbeck described the poverty and dangers faced by workers. The novels of Ernest Hemingway and F. Scott Fitzgerald wrote of people in search of adventure and escape. William Faulkner set his widely acclaimed novels in Mississippi. Willa Cather was one of the first U.S. novelists to create strong female characters.

Meanwhile—during what became known as the Harlem Renaissance—the African American community created a distinct literary voice. Black writers drew on a tradition founded in large part by W. E. B. Du Bois, a renowned essayist and thinker born just after the Civil War. In the 1920s, the writings of James Weldon Johnson, Langston Hughes, and Jean Toomer appealed to whites as well as blacks. In the 1930s and 1940s, Richard Wright examined racial discrimination, while Zora Neale Hurston drew on folklore from the Caribbean and the southern United States.

Richard Wright

In the 1950s and 1960s, Jack Kerouac and Allen Ginsberg broke new ground with free-flowing prose and poetry. The African American authors Ralph Ellison and James Baldwin probed black identity in the United States. Saul Bellow and Philip Roth described the Jewish experience in North America.

During the second half of the twentieth century, female and Native American authors reached a broad audience. Betty Friedan's works helped to launch the woman's rights movement of the 1970s. The Sioux writer Vine Deloria Jr. examined the plight of Native Americans. In the 1980s, graphic novels emerged from the tradition of popular comic books.

Many popular U.S. authors work in the genre of historical fiction. Charles Frazier's *Cold Mountain* is the tale of a Civil War survivor who treks through a chaotic southern landscape. Geraldine Brooks borrowed a character from Louisa May Alcott's *Little Women* to write her novel *March*, which won the Pulitzer Prize for fiction in 2006. *The Known World* by Edward P. Jones explores the subject of Virginia slave owners—both black and white.

▶ Art and Media

Before Europeans arrived, Native American artists were working in a variety of forms and materials. Pottery, weapons, tools, blankets, jewelry, and clothing displayed distinctive geometric designs. In eastern forests, weavers used bark, branches, and reeds to make baskets and adornments. Rock painting was a common art form in the southwestern desert. In the northwestern Pacific, wood-carvers carved tall totem poles, depicting gods, important people, and memorable events from massive tree trunks.

In the nineteenth and early twentieth centuries, images of cowboys and Native Americans on the western frontier captivated the nation. George Catlin toured North America, portraying Indians and their ways of life. Charles Marion Russell, a former ranch hand, painted cowboys and cattle. Frederic Remington, famous for his sculpture and painting, created memorable images of the western frontier.

James Whistler was best known for subtle portraits. Although born to American parents, John Singer Sargent lived in Europe. European tradition inspired his portraits and landscapes. Winslow Homer began as an illustrator for newspapers and journals. He used oil and watercolors to paint detailed scenes of seacoasts and the natural world.

In New York, the style of abstract expressionism enabled artists to convey their ideas with color, shapes, and lines. The movement started after World War II and brought into the limelight Jackson Pollock and Mark Rothko. In the early 1960s, Andy Warhol became the leader of the pop art movement. Pop art painters elevated everyday items, such as soup cans, to the level of artistic symbols.

Jackson Pollock

Many well-known artists of the early twenty-first century mix the media of painting, film, video, photography, and computer imagery. Cindy Sherman has created thousands of photographic self-portraits, using a variety of settings and characters. Installation artists, including Judy Chicago and Sandy Skoglund, build striking three-dimensional environments using light, sculpture, and sound.

New York, Chicago, and Los Angeles are the leading centers for professional theater in the United States. The nation's noteworthy

Chicagoan **Oprah Winfrey** *(left)* is a successful television talk show hostess. She is also known for her philanthropy in the twenty-first century. Another star in Chicago is Millennium Park. It features some striking additions to the city's famous public art, such as the Crown Fountain. It is made up of two 50-foot (15.2 m) glass blocks separated by a shallow reflecting pool. Changing lights and video images of Chicagoans make the **Crown Fountain** stand out. Water pours from the top of each block from mid-spring to mid-fall. Work on Millennium Park began in 1996.

playwrights include Eugene O'Neill, Tennessee Williams, Arthur Miller, Lillian Hellman, Edward Albee, and August Wilson. A tradition of musical theater remained strong in the early twenty-first century. Jonathan Larson wrote the music and lyrics for *Rent*, a show that ran for thousands of performances after it opened in 1996. The stage version of *The Lion King*, a 1994 Disney animated film, opened in Minneapolis in 1997 and soon moved to New York where it is still drawing crowds. The production won a total of six Tony Awards in 1998, including Best Play and Best Director.

American movies became big business in the early twentieth century. Modern U.S. filmmakers export their works around the world, and the lives and work of big Hollywood stars are familiar to nearly everyone. The directors John Ford, Woody Allen, Martin Scorsese, and Quentin Tarantino all broke new ground in film style and content. Mel Gibson raised controversy with historical films such as *Braveheart*, *The Passion of the Christ*, and *Apocalypto*. Sofia Coppola, daughter of renowned movie director Francis Ford Coppola, made the award-winning *Lost in Translation*, a film about the clash of U.S. and Japanese lifestyles.

In the mid-twentieth century, television became the most popular entertainment and information medium in the United States. Millions of viewers tune in to modern television dramas such as *The Sopranos, Six Feet Under, Grey's Anatomy, 24,* and *Deadwood*. Specialized cable television networks cover sports, travel, and food. Daytime TV hosts such as Oprah Winfrey deal with social and personal issues on their shows.

Music

Jazz, the blues, country and western, and rock and roll all originated in the United States. Jazz developed from dance tunes, work chants, and blues songs performed in the South, particularly in New Orleans. Louis Armstrong, Duke Ellington, and Ella Fitzgerald were accomplished jazz artists. Albert King and Billie Holiday sang the blues. Elvis Presley and Chuck Berry defined early rock and roll. Jimi Hendrix and Janis Joplin were leading rock stars of the 1960s. In the next decade, punk rock arrived on the scene from Great Britain. In the 1990s, Kurt Cobain and Nirvana developed their own sound from this influence. Among modern country-and-western singers, Garth Brooks, Alan Jackson, and the Dixie Chicks stand out. The group Nine Inch Nails helped create industrial rock, combining traditional rock ensembles with computer-generated sounds.

A new style of sung poetry gave birth to rap and hip-hop music in the late 1970s. African American and Latino artists, dancers, singers, and disc

A MUSICAL MELTING POT

Zydeco is the music of the Cajuns of Louisiana, a people descended from French settlers who came to the South from Nova Scotia, Canada, in the mid-1800s. Zydeco mixes African American blues with French Canadian folk music. The bands include accordion, washboard, violin, bass, guitar, and drums. The first zydeco records were made in the 1920s. A generation later, younger Cajun musicians borrowed musical styles from country and western and rhythm and blues, added a piano and horns, and created the new genre of swamp pop–still popular in Louisiana, Texas, Britain, Europe, and Japan.

jockeys contributed to this new style. Hip-hop artists combined rhythmic bass and drum tracks with inventive rhyming lyrics. By the early twenty-first century, groups around the world were imitating the style of rappers, such as Run DMC, Tupac Shakur, and Mos Def.

Sports

The favorite organized sports in the United States are baseball, football, basketball, and hockey. Most large cities have at least one professional team. Millions of fans follow pro sports leagues on television and radio. Dwyane Wade, Yao Ming, and Allen Iverson, accomplished basketball players, are international stars. Professional baseball teams developed Latin American star players such as Fernando Valenzuela, Alex Rodriguez, and Sammy Sosa. In the early twenty-first century, Japanese players including Ichiro Suzuki and Hideki "Godzilla" Matsui are also making their mark in American professional baseball.

New York Yankees third baseman Alex Rodriguez bats against the Tampa Bay Devil Rays on April 2, 2007. The Yankees won the game by a score of 9 to 5.

The Internet is filled with information about cultural life in the United States. To learn more about its food, sports, music, literature, films, and visual arts, go to www.vgsbooks.com for links.

Fans also enjoy watching high school and college-level competition. Nonprofessional athletes play baseball and softball on sandlots throughout the country. Climate often determines what sporting activities are most popular in a region. Most northern local parks, for example, offer indoor and outdoor hockey arenas. Hiking and skiing are common pastimes in mountainous areas, while surfing is big on the Pacific coast and in Hawaii.

Young people from throughout the nation compete on school soccer teams. The United States fields a team in the World Cup, an international soccer championship, and also hosts a professional league. Amateur athletes also train to compete in the Olympics—international sporting events held in summers and winters every four years.

Food

From its earliest history, American cuisine has drawn on local crops and the ethnic foods that arrived with its many immigrant communities. The country's vast stretches of fertile land provide a bounty of fruits, vegetables, grains, and livestock for meat. Native American foods adopted by the early United States include corn, beans, potatoes, squash, and game meat, including turkey, venison, and bison. In later years, popular European dishes became American icons: apple pie, pizza, hot dogs, and hamburgers.

Regional cuisines have emerged throughout the country. French immigrants and African Americans contributed to a distinctive southern cuisine. Mexican food, once popular in Texas and the Southwest, has spread throughout the country. In the twentieth century, Asian cooking techniques became popular on the Pacific coast. This gave rise to fusion cuisine that combines classic American ingredients with cooking techniques from China and Japan. Large urban areas host a variety of ethnic restaurants offering cuisine once nearly unknown in the United States, from Africa, South Asia, South America, and the Middle East.

People in the United States eat breakfasts that may include eggs, bread, fruit, cereals, coffee, juice, and milk. Lunches are light meals eaten quickly in the middle of the working day. They may include soup, salad, a sandwich, or portable food that can be moved from shop to office or home. The traditional evening dinner has

JAMBALAYA

This renowned dish is famous in Louisiana, particularly in New Orleans, which is said to be home to some of the best restaurants in the United States. Jambalaya is a hot stew of rice, vegetables, spices, and meat or fish that blends French, African, and Caribbean cooking styles.

1 lb. hot sausage, chopped

½ chicken, cut

2 big yellow onions, chopped fine

1 to 2 crushed garlic cloves

4 c. water

pinch of salt, pepper, red pepper, and onion powder

1 bell pepper, chopped

2 banana peppers, chopped

1 bundle green onions, chopped

2 c. uncooked rice

1. Brown sausage and chicken and put them aside.
2. Fry yellow onions and garlic while constantly stirring.
3. Add meat and water to cover.
4. Season to taste with salt, pepper, red pepper, and onion powder, and cook until meat is tender.
5. Add peppers and green onions, then rice.
6. Simmer for 15 minutes, or until the rice is cooked.
7. Turn the rice over once, to bring the bottom layer to the top. Leave over low heat until all the water has evaporated and the rice is tender. Serve with French bread, white beans, and green salad.

Serves 4 to 5

several courses, with meat or fish, vegetables, and side dishes, followed by a dessert.

In recent years, American food and diet have come under close scrutiny. The traditional cooking styles and large portions create a diet high in calories, fat, and sugar, leading to health problems and obesity. In addition, the popular fast food bought at restaurants and shops has little nutritional value. In reaction, vegetarian and raw food diets are increasingly popular.

Holidays and Festivals

The United States has a wide variety of public holidays. The first of these is Independence Day, celebrating the signing of the Declaration of Independence on July 4. The Thanksgiving holiday, on the last Thursday of November, is a remembrance of a meal shared by English settlers and Native Americans in colonial times. Flag Day takes place on June 14. Veterans Day, honoring military veterans, occurs on November 11. Memorial Day, the final Monday in May, is another salute to war veterans and those who have died in battle.

More recent civic holidays include Martin Luther King Day, on January 15, in celebration of the civil rights leader's birthday. Presidents' Day occurs in February, the month of the birthdays of Abraham Lincoln and George Washington. Cinco de Mayo honors a Mexican victory in battle on May 5. The Labor Day holiday falls on the first Monday of September.

Religious holidays include Easter and Christmas, both Christian holidays. On December 26, the seven-day holiday of Kwanzaa begins. This festival of African American heritage originated in the United States. Jews celebrate the holy days of Rosh Hashanah and Yom Kippur. Families with roots in China and some other Asian societies observe an annual new year festival in late January. Muslims fast and assemble to hear prayers during the holy month of Ramadan.

Many visitors make a special trip to the **Vietnam Veterans Memorial in Washington, D.C.** for Memorial Day or Veteran's Day. U.S. soldiers killed in the Vietnam War are listed on this huge black granite wall. A registry near the wall helps family and friends find their loved one's name.

THE ECONOMY

The United States developed the world's largest economy in the twentieth century. The modern United States has an annual gross domestic product (GDP) of more than $13 trillion. The GDP measures the worth of all goods and services produced within the country in one year. The economy is growing at about 3 percent every year.

But the United States still faces intense competition with foreign nations. In the early 1990s, U.S. leaders passed the North American Free Trade Agreement (NAFTA). This helped to lift trade barriers between the United States, Canada, and Mexico. The treaty ended the payment of tariffs (taxes) by companies in member-nations on imports and exports.

The end of tariffs, the falling cost of transport, and cheap labor in nations such as China have allowed many foreign companies to compete with their U.S. rivals. The result has been the loss of manufacturing and factory jobs in many states.

Nearly all U.S. businesses are in private hands. There are few controls on investment. The U.S. government, however, does play a role. Over the

years, the government has passed laws to prevent monopolies. It also sets the minimum wage employers can pay to their workers. Some federal laws strive to assure safe working conditions and prevent environmental damage.

○ Services

The service industry in the United States makes up the largest single sector of the economy. Service businesses employ about 78 percent of the workforce and contribute about 77 percent of gross domestic product. These companies provide banking, insurance, hotel and motel, and transportation services. Restaurants and retail stores provide goods and services to their customers.

The large service industry developed in the twentieth century. With more leisure time and more money to spend, people sought to make their lives more comfortable and convenient. While banking and insurance have been around for centuries, new services arose in the twentieth century to fill more specific needs. These include health care, child care, delivery, business consulting, entertainment, animal training, travel guides, translators, and home repairs. In the twenty-first century, telecommunications and Internet services were the fastest-growing service businesses.

Manufacturing and Trade

Manufacturing accounts for about 20 percent of the country's GDP and employs about 19 percent of the workforce. Major industrial centers are in the northeastern and midwestern United States. A growing number of factories operate in southern states and along the Pacific coast.

California and Washington specialize in making food products and high-tech goods, such as aircraft, aerospace equipment, computers, and computer software. Older factories in the Great Lakes area furnish much of the nation's iron, steel, and automobiles. Textile mills, food-processing plants, and printing firms concentrated in the northeastern and southeastern United States. Oil refineries and petrochemical businesses are based mainly in mineral-producing states, including Texas and Louisiana.

Of all manufactured goods, transportation equipment—such as cars, trucks, and aircraft—make up the largest sector. Food products and beverages, chemicals, machinery, metals, printed materials, petroleum, and coal are other leading moneymakers.

The **underground Mathies coal mine in western Pennsylvania** got busy when the price of coal doubled in 2001. More than one thousand laid-off miners returned to work that year.

Because of the size of its industrial economy, the United States is the world's most active trading nation. Its primary trading partners are Canada, Japan, Mexico, Britain, and Germany. Major exports are chemicals, motor vehicles and parts, computers, grains, and industrial machinery. Imports include motor vehicles and parts, petroleum, clothing, toys, and metals such as iron and steel.

The United States has run a trade deficit since the 1970s. This means the country imports more goods than it sells abroad. Trade issues between the United States and China came to the fore in the early twenty-first century. By paying much lower wages, Chinese companies compete effectively with U.S. manufacturers. As a result, the United States runs an ever-larger trade deficit with China. As the Chinese economy expands, that country is becoming an economic, political, and military rival of the United States.

Mining and Energy

Mining contributes 1 percent to the nation's GDP and employs about 0.5 percent of the workforce. Important minerals include copper, gold, granite, iron ore, limestone, phosphate rock, and salt. Petroleum, natural gas, and coal are the most important energy sectors.

HERE COMES THE SMART CAR

The Smart Car began in Europe. It was first called the Swatchmobile. The car was only 98 inches (249 cm) long. Drivers could park it nose first to the curb. They could also fit two Smart Cars in a single, average parking space.

A California company called ZAP (for Zero Air Pollution) will begin selling the Smart Car in the United States. The car will run on electricity. Owners take five or six hours to charge the Smart Car from an ordinary household outlet. The car will reach a top speed of 85 miles (137 km) an hour.

Some people worry the little Smart Car will be unsafe. It weighs less than 1 ton (1 metric ton) and much less than the big Humvee H2 (more than 3 tons, or 3 metric tons). But it also may help big cities reduce pollution, overcrowded streets, and a lack of parking space.

Privately owned mining companies drill for oil in Alaska, Texas, California and from onshore and offshore wells along the Gulf of Mexico. Miners extract much of the nation's coal in the Appalachians and Wyoming. Nevada yields the most gold.

The United States is the world's second-largest producer of petroleum, but the country is the single greatest consumer of this limited resource. The United States must import about 30 percent of the oil it needs.

A limited global oil supply has led researchers to explore alternative fuel sources, such as solar energy and wind power. Scientists have also developed methods to convert other energy-producing resources—including coal, oil shale, and bituminous sands—into synthetic oils. Ethanol, which is made from corn and other crops, is becoming another alternative source for automotive fuel. Automakers have also brought hybrid cars to the market. These vehicles run on electric power as well as petroleum.

Vehicles, factories, and homes consume a vast amount of energy in the United States. Petroleum meets about 40 percent of the demand, while coal and natural gas each contribute about 25 percent. Nuclear and hydroelectric power plants account for the remaining 10 percent. Major hydroelectric projects in the United States include the Hoover Dam along the Arizona-Nevada border. The huge structure diverts the Colorado River to supply energy and water to Arizona, Nevada, and California. The Grand Coulee Dam, on the Columbia River in Washington State, is the greatest single source of waterpower in the United States.

Agriculture

About 98 percent of U.S. territory is rural. Yet less than 25 percent of the country's population lives in rural areas. Farming employs just 1.6 percent of the workforce. Although the United States creates only 1 percent of its GDP from farming, the nation leads the world in agricultural output. Farms and ranches in the United States supply about half of the world's corn, 20 percent of its meat, and just over 10 percent of its wheat.

Hoover Dam

Farmers benefit from large tracts of fertile land, up-to-date machinery, and modern methods of cultivation. But the high costs of keeping up with current technology—as well as some modern farming

This field in Big Rock, Illinois, is planted with **soybeans.**

methods—is changing agriculture. Since the early twentieth century, the number of small, family-owned farms in the United States has steadily decreased. Meanwhile, the number of large, corporate-run farms has increased.

At 825,000 acres (334,000 hectares), the King Ranch in southern Texas covers land in six counties, making it the largest ranch in the United States. The ranch owners raise quarter horses and thoroughbred horses, more than sixty thousand head of cattle, and thousands of acres of feed. Oranges grow on King Ranch property in Florida. The ranch has also set aside large swaths of land as wildlife preserves.

The country's leading farm products are beef, milk, corn, soybeans, poultry, eggs, hogs, wheat, and cotton. Ranchers and farmers in the Great Plains raise most of the nation's beef cattle, wheat, and corn. Dairy cattle, grains, and potatoes are grown on farms throughout the Central Lowlands. Tobacco and peanuts thrive in the warm climate of the southern states. Vegetables and citrus fruits are key exports of Florida, California, and Hawaii.

Forestry and Fishing

The United States is one of the world's leading producers of timber. Woodlands cover about one-third of the country. The largest tracts are in Alaska and in the western United States. The U.S. government has set aside about two-thirds of the nation's forested land for commercial use. Forest products include lumber, pulp, turpentine, wood tar, and rosin (a natural resin used to make varnish and other goods).

Since colonial times, farmers and developers have cleared forests to create farmland and urban areas. To guarantee a steady supply of timber, foresters manage government-owned timberlands. Workers use different methods of harvesting and replanting to get the maximum amount of timber, while maintaining a healthy forest for future supplies.

Employees in forestry and fishing make up about 0.9 percent of the workforce. These industries contribute about 1 percent to the nation's GDP. Commercial fishers in the United States harvest about 5.5 million tons (5 million metric tons) of fish and shellfish annually. The largest catches, mainly oysters, shrimps, and menhaden, come from the Gulf of Mexico. Crews in the Pacific Ocean net a variety of fish and shellfish, including cod, crab, salmon, and tuna.

Water pollution and overfishing have damaged some of the nation's fishing grounds. The United States sets strict quotas for certain species. It also limits the number of fishing vessels that can operate in overfished areas.

Transportation and Tourism

People in the United States rely heavily on private cars for transportation. About 215 million cars are in use, and the country has nearly 3.9 million miles (6.3 million km) of roads, including 1.6 million miles (2.6 million km) of unpaved roads. Crisscrossing the United States is a vast network of interstate highways that links major cities.

The United States has 141,961 miles (228,464 km) of railroad track. Most U.S. railroad companies earn the bulk of their income from hauling cargo. But many people, especially in the northeastern United States, rely on commuter trains to get to and from work. Other travel by passenger train began to disappear in the 1950s and 1960s as buses, cars, and airplanes became commonplace.

In the nation's largest metropolitan areas, commuter trains and subways carry commuters in and out of town. But the most widely used form of urban public transportation is the bus. Several U.S. cities have built light-rail transit (LRT) systems. These are electric-powered systems that run in dense urban areas. Boston, San Francisco, Los Angeles, Portland, and San Diego have the nation's busiest LRT systems.

About fifty ports—on U.S. waterways and coasts—handle 15 percent of the nation's freight. Many freighters and ships on the Mississippi River system enter the Great Lakes by way of the port of Chicago on Lake Michigan.

Airports are near every sizable U.S. city. There are more than five thousand paved runways and more than two hundred airlines. Private companies operate all public air traffic in the United States, including

The first light-rail line in Minneapolis, Minnesota, went into service in December 2004. It connects downtown sports arenas with the airport and popular shopping areas such as the Mall of America in Bloomington, Minnesota.

freight and passenger flights. Regional hubs provide local services, and most of the larger airports handle international traffic. In 2005 the Hartsfield-Jackson Atlanta International Airport became the world's busiest airport.

Nearly 40 million tourists from all over the world visit the United States every year. These vacationers pump $40 billion into the U.S. economy. The largest numbers of visitors come from Canada, Mexico, and Japan. World-famous museums, cultural performances, and landmarks draw about 17 million people every year to New York City—one of the world's most visited cities. The beaches and warm weather of Florida, California, and Hawaii have made these states major U.S. tourism centers for anglers, scuba divers, and sunbathers. In California and Florida, amusement parks entertain millions every year.

The rugged terrain of Oregon, Washington, Montana, Idaho, and Colorado challenges mountain climbers and hikers. Resorts in the Rocky Mountains and in the Sierra Nevada attract skiers of all skill

The Lower Falls *(left)* in Yellowstone National Park, Wyoming, drops about 308 ft. (94 m) to the bottom of the Grand Canyon of the Yellowstone River. The canyon is rusting. Its unusual colors come from iron heated by geysers and exposed to the weather.

levels. At national parks, such as Yellowstone, Yosemite, Grand Teton, and Grand Canyon, campers enjoy scenic wildernesses, some of which have been protected by federal law for more than a century.

Communications

The United States has developed a busy communications sector. There are more than 350 million telephones in use, a majority of them mobile phones. Personal computers have become commonplace in homes. About 185 million people subscribe to Internet services. This is the highest percentage of Internet users in the world.

Information media are abundant as well. About half the population reads daily newspapers. The leading national newspapers are the *New York Times*, the *Wall Street Journal*, the *Washington Post*, and *USA Today*. U.S. companies publish about 100,000 books each year. Radios are present in 99 percent of all homes, and households possess an average of 2.5 televisions each. Cable television services operate throughout the country, offering a broad menu of information and entertainment programs.

The Future

The United States is among the most advanced and stable nations in the world. This standing has enabled the country's citizens to achieve a high standard of living. The United States has also become a major force in the global marketplace. International trade agreements help U.S. corporations compete worldwide.

The United States has troubling issues within its borders, however, including crime, poverty, pollution, illegal immigration, and public health. Abroad, it remains entangled in civil conflict in Iraq. The invasion of Iraq sparked criticism of the use of U.S. military power to influence foreign countries.

Some believe the United States should help and force, if necessary, other nations to adopt free markets and democracy. Others believe the country should avoid conflicts overseas. The proper use of military power and political pressure abroad is a debate that will continue in the future.

> Catch up on current events in the United States. Go to www.vgsbooks.com for links to the latest news.

Timeline

CA. 22,000 B.C. Nomads cross a land bridge between north-eastern Asia and North America.

CA. 1000 The Mound Builder culture thrives along the Mississippi Valley region.

1492 Italian explorer Christopher Columbus arrives in the Bahamas.

1513 The Spanish captain Ponce de Leon explores Florida.

1540s Francisco Coronado explores the western mountains and southern Great Plains of North America.

1565 The Spanish found Saint Augustine, Florida, the first permanent European settlement in the United States.

1585 The English build a settlement at Roanoke, near the Outer Banks of North Carolina.

1607 English settlers found Jamestown, in the colony of Virginia.

1620 English Pilgrims land at Plymouth Rock, Massachusetts.

1624 The Dutch establish the colony of New Netherland.

1754 The French and Indian War breaks out on the western frontier.

1775 Colonists and British soldiers skirmish at Concord and Lexington, Massachusetts.

1776 The Second Continental Congress passes the Declaration of Independence.

1781 The Articles of Confederation set up a federal government in the American colonies.

1783 The Treaty of Paris ends the Revolutionary War and recognizes the independent United States of America.

1787 Leaders of the former colonies gather to write the U.S. Constitution.

1803 The U.S. government pays $15 million to France for the Louisiana Purchase, which includes lands from the Mississippi River to the Rocky Mountains.

1812 The War of 1812 breaks out between Great Britain and the United States.

1848 The Mexican-American War ends in a U.S. victory and the Treaty of Guadalupe Hidalgo. The treaty grants parts of Texas, Arizona, New Mexico, Colorado, California, and Utah to the United States.

1861 The Civil War begins between North (Union) and South (Confederacy) over the issue of states' rights and slavery.

1863 President Abraham Lincoln issues the Emancipation Proclamation, legally ending slavery.

1865   The South surrenders, and the Civil War ends. John Wilkes
       Booth assassinates President Lincoln in Washington, D.C.

1867   The United States buys Alaska from Russia.

1898   The United States defeats Spain in the Spanish-American War and wins
       possession of Puerto Rico, Cuba, Guam, and the Philippines.

1917   The United States enters World War I and sends troops to fight alongside the
       British and French. In the next year, the war ends with a victory against Germany.

1919   The Eighteenth Amendment to the Constitution bars the sale or possession of
       alcohol. (It was repealed by the Twenty-First Amendment in 1933.)

1920   The Nineteenth Amendment grants women the right to vote.

1929   The New York Stock Exchange crashes, setting off the Great Depression.

1941   Japan bombs Pearl Harbor on December 7, bringing the United States into World War II
       against Italy, Japan, and Germany. World War II ends with the surrender of Germany
       and Japan in 1945.

1963   President John F. Kennedy is assassinated in Dallas, Texas.

1964   Congress passes the Civil Rights Act.

1969   The United States lands two astronauts on the surface of the moon.

1973   America pulls out of South Vietnam after more than eleven years of military, economic
       and political support of the armed conflict there. Inventor Martin Cooper makes the
       first mobile cell phone call.

1974   President Richard Nixon resigns from office after a political scandal.

1976   Author Saul Bellow wins the Nobel Prize in Literature.

1991   To turn back Iraq's invasion of Kuwait, the U.S. mounts a successful invasion and
       defeats the Iraqi army.

2001   Terrorists hijack four passenger jets. They fly two planes into the World Trade Center
       in New York City and a third into the Pentagon outside Washington, D.C. The fourth
       plane crashes into a Pennsylvania field. The attacks kill more than three thousand
       people.

2003   The United States invades Iraq and overthrows the regime of Saddam Hussein.

2005   Hurricane Katrina devastates the Gulf of Mexico coast, including New Orleans.

2006   Keith Ellison of Minnesota becomes the first Muslim elected to the U.S.
       House of Representatives.

2007   The city of Chicago applies to host the 2016 Summer Olympic
       Games.

COUNTRY NAME United States of America

AREA 3.8 million square miles (9.8 million sq. km)

MAIN LANDFORMS Atlantic Coastal Plain, Appalachian Mountains, Mississippi River valley, Great Plains, Intermountain Region, Central Lowlands, Cordillera, Rocky Mountains

HIGHEST POINT Mount McKinley (Denali), 20,320 feet (6,194 m)

MAJOR RIVERS Hudson, Ohio, Mississippi, Missouri, Colorado, Columbia

ANIMALS Alligators, bald eagles, bears, beavers, bison, bobcats, condors, coyotes, cranes, deer, dolphins, egrets, herons, ibis, loons, mallards, manatees, panthers, turtles, racoons, squirrels, whales

CAPITAL CITY Washington, D.C. (District of Columbia)

OTHER MAJOR CITIES New York, Los Angeles, Chicago, Houston, Philadelphia, Phoenix, San Antonio, San Diego, Dallas, San Jose, Detroit, Indianapolis, Jacksonville, San Francisco, Columbus, Austin, Memphis, Baltimore, Fort Worth, Charlotte, Denver, Minneapolis

OFFICIAL LANGUAGE None

MONETARY UNIT Dollar. 1 dollar = 100 cents

UNITED STATES CURRENCY

The dollar is the official currency of the United States. In the eighteenth century, the British colonists of North America used the Spanish dollar and the taler, a currency of the Holy Roman Empire. After independence, the new nation declared the dollar as the new currency. The United States has a one-dollar coin and coins of 1, 5, 10, 25, and 50 cents.

Dollars have circulated as a paper currency since 1862. The modern one-dollar note carries a portrait of George Washington, painted by Gilbert Stuart. On the reverse side is the Great Seal of the United States. It carries the signatures of the secretary of the Treasury and the treasurer of the United States. There are also notes in denominations of 5, 10, 20, 50, and 100 dollars in circulation.

Currency Fast Facts

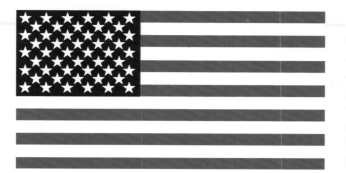

The Continental Congress adopted the Stars and Stripes on June 14, 1776. The flag had thirteen white stars on a blue field, and five red and four white stripes. The stars represented the thirteen American colonies. The stripes came from the flag of the Sons of Liberty, a group seeking independence from Great Britain. In 1794, when two new states joined the union, two stars and two stripes were added. In 1795 Congress raised the number of stripes to fifteen. In 1818 the number of stripes was set permanently at thirteen. A new star would be added to the flag for every state that joined the union. In 1814 the poet Francis Scott Key first called the flag the Star-Spangled Banner, another popular nickname for the U.S. flag. This became the title of the national anthem, set to Key's poem of the same name.

"The Star-Spangled Banner" is the national anthem of the United States. Francis Scott Key, a lawyer and poet from Maryland, wrote the poem during the War of 1812. In September 1814, Key found himself held by the British aboard a prisoners' boat in Baltimore harbor. From the boat, he witnessed a nighttime British bombardment of Fort McHenry. The next morning, the U.S. flag was still waving over the fort. The sight inspired him to write "The Star-Spangled Banner." Key printed the poem soon afterward and set it to the music of a popular British song, "To Anacreon in Heaven." In 1931 the U.S. Congress officially adopted "The Star-Spangled Banner" as the national anthem. Although the poem has four verses, musical groups and singers usually perform only the first verse:

> Oh! Say, can you see, by the dawn's early light,
> What so proudly we hailed at the twilight's last gleaming,
> Whose broad stripes and bright stars, thro' the perilous fight,
> O'er the ramparts we watched were so gallantly streaming?
> And the rockets' red glare, the bombs bursting in air,
> Gave proof thro' the night that our flag was still there;
> Oh! Say, does that star-spangled banner yet wave
> O'er the land of the free and the home of the brave?

 Listen to the United States' national anthem. Go to www.vgsbooks .com for a link.

Flag National Anthem

MUHAMMAD ALI (b. 1942) A champion heavyweight boxer, Muhammad Ali was born Cassius Clay in Louisville, Kentucky. He won a boxing gold medal at the Olympic Games in 1960. Afterward, he converted to Islam and changed his name. He resisted being drafted into the military during the Vietnam War, saying fighting in the war would be against his religion. Although he won a Supreme Court appeal, he was stripped of his heavyweight crown.

HILLARY RODHAM CLINTON (b. 1947) A leading political figure and U.S. senator, Hillary Clinton was born in Chicago. She attended Wellesley College and Yale Law School. She worked as a lawyer in Little Rock, Arkansas, after marrying Bill Clinton, who would become governor of that state. She became First Lady after Clinton won the presidential election of 1992. She was elected senator from New York in 2000. In 2007 she announced she would run for president in 2008.

ANGELINA JOLIE (b. 1975) Actress Angelina Jolie was born in Los Angeles. The daughter of Jon Voigt, a Hollywood actor, Jolie appeared with her father in her first film when she was seven. In 2000 she won an Academy Award as a supporting actress in *Girl, Interrupted*.

MARTIN LUTHER KING JR. (1929–1968) A civil rights leader born in Atlanta, Georgia, King began his career as a Baptist pastor in Montgomery, Alabama. He led a boycott of that city's bus system after Rosa Parks, a Montgomery resident, refused to give up her seat to a white person. In 1963 King led a March on Washington to appeal for equal civil rights for African Americans and made the famous "I have a dream" speech that roused many in the United States to support his cause. He was assassinated in Memphis in 1968.

NANCY PELOSI (b. 1940) Born in Baltimore, Nancy Pelosi became the first woman Speaker of the House of Representatives in 2006. The daughter of a congressman, she was first elected to the House of Representatives in 1987, representing San Francisco, California.

EDGAR ALLAN POE (1809–1849) A poet, journalist, and short story author, Poe was born in Boston, the son of poor actors. Orphaned at a young age, he was adopted by John Allan of Richmond, Virginia. He struggled to earn a living as a journalist in New York City and began writing reviews and short stories for several journals. Poe's most famous stories, including "The Tell-Tale Heart," "The Fall of the House of Usher," and "The Black Cat," detail strange and macabre events. His most famous poem is "The Raven."

COLIN POWELL (b. 1937) Powell was born to Jamaican immigrants in New York City. He served two tours of duty during the Vietnam War. In 1989 he reached the rank of four-star general and became chairman of the Joint Chiefs of Staff, the highest position in the military. He was the first African American to serve as secretary of state, a job he held from 2001 through 2005.

CONDOLEEZA RICE (b. 1954) Born in Birmingham, Alabama, Condoleeza Rice is a scholar, musician, and political figure. As a child, she experienced violence firsthand as African Americans fought for their civil rights in Birmingham. She was a professor of political science at Stanford University during the 1990s. In 2005 she succeeded Colin Powell as secretary of state. Rice is the first African American woman to hold this high office.

SACAGAWEA (CA. 1787–1812) Sacagawea, born in Idaho, was a Native American and member of the Shoshone Nation. She was kidnapped at the age of eleven and taken to North Dakota, where she married a French trapper. Explorers William Clark and Meriwether Lewis hired her to interpret for them during their western voyage.

SITTING BULL (CA. 1831–1890) A Lakota chief, Sitting Bull was born in South Dakota. He led battles against the U.S. cavalry at Killdeer Mountain in 1864 and at the Battle of the Little Bighorn in 1876. After this victory, Sitting Bull led his people into Canada. In 1881 he surrendered and returned to the United States. He was killed while being arrested by cavalry soldiers in 1890.

MARK TWAIN (1835–1910) Author of famous novels, short stories, and nonfiction essays, Mark Twain was born Samuel Langhorne Clemens in Florida, Missouri. After the Civil War, he worked as a newspaper editor and journalist. His best-known books include *The Adventures of Tom Sawyer, The Adventures of Huckleberry Finn, Life on the Mississippi,* and *A Connecticut Yankee in King Arthur's Court.*

VENUS WILLIAMS (b. 1980) A professional tennis player, Venus Williams was born in Lynwood, California. She is the older sister of Serena Williams. Both sisters have been ranked No. 1, and both have won several major Grand Slam tournaments, which include the Australian Open, the French Open, the U.S. Open, and Wimbledon.

OPRAH WINFREY (b. 1954) A popular television personality, Winfrey was born in Kosciusko, Mississippi. In 1984 she began hosting a talk show in Chicago. *The Oprah Winfrey Show* was soon broadcast nationwide and became the number one television talk show.

ELDRICK "TIGER" WOODS (b. 1975) Born in Cypress, California, Tiger Woods began playing golf at the age of two. In 1994 he was the youngest golfer to win the U.S. Amateur Championship. He became the world's leading professional golfer soon after leaving Stanford University.

BANZAI PIPELINE (EHUKAI BEACH) This world-famous surfing beach is on the north shore of the island of Oahu, Hawaii. The towering waves can reach more than three stories high and crash at high speed onto a sea bottom made of jagged coral.

GRAND CANYON A 200-mile (322 km) gorge, it runs across northern Arizona, carved by the Colorado River. In some places, the gorge is more than 1 mile (1.6 km) deep. The river has carved a gigantic maze of steep cliffs, beautiful mesas, and towering pillars.

GRAND OLE OPRY HOUSE This theater in Nashville, Tennessee, hosts a world-famous country music radio show every Saturday. The Opry started as the *WSM Barn Dance* show in the 1920s and has since featured thousands of country music stars.

GREAT SMOKY MOUNTAINS This national park crosses the border between Tennessee and North Carolina. On many days, a wispy haze covers the mountain tops, home to black bear, deer, fox, and many other species. Hikers can enjoy a large network of trails and campsites scattered through the park or raft and canoe on the swift-flowing mountain streams.

KENAI FJORDS NATIONAL PARK This park lies on the Kenai Peninsula along the Pacific coast of southern Alaska. The Harding Icefield, the largest ice field in North America, covers 300 square miles (777 sq. km).

MOUNT RUSHMORE This famous monument in the Black Hills of western South Dakota shows the heads of four U.S. presidents: Washington, Jefferson, Lincoln, and Theodore Roosevelt. The sculptor Gutzon Borglum carved the heads from a 60-foot (18 m) cliff face.

MOUNT SAINT HELENS NATIONAL VOLCANIC MONUMENT A park is created around an active volcano that last erupted in 1980, destroying 230 square miles (596 sq. km) of surrounding forest and spewing ash and smoke thousands of miles. Visitors may climb the volcano's slopes and explore the land as it slowly regenerates itself.

ROCK AND ROLL HALL OF FAME The museum, in downtown Cleveland, Ohio, honors rock artists. The hall has exhibits on singers, songwriters, instrumentalists, record producers, sidemen, disc jockeys, and journalists.

WASHINGTON, D.C. The capital city of the United States, the city is home to the Capitol Building, the White House, and several imposing monuments along the Mall, a grassy rectangle in the city's center. Tourists visit the somber Vietnam Veterans memorial, which has the names of the American dead carved in black marble. Other sights to see are the Lincoln Memorial, the Jefferson Memorial, the Holocaust Museum, the National Air and Space Museum, and the Smithsonian Museum.

abolitionist: a person who works to end slavery

amendment: a change in a law or to the U.S. Constitution

archipelago: a group of islands, such as the Hawaiian Archipelago

bicameral: divided into two chambers, as in the U.S. Congress and many state legislatures

Cold War: the rivalry between the United States and the Soviet Union after World War II

cordillera: a range of mountains in the western United States

Harlem Renaissance: a movement of African American writing and art that reached its peak during the 1920s

Louisiana Purchase: a transaction in 1803 that added 828,000 square miles (2.1 million sq. km) of new land to the western United States

New Deal: a series of government programs to relieve poverty and unemployment during the Great Depression of the 1930s

Paleo-Indians: the original inhabitants of the North American continent, who began arriving about twenty thousand years ago

Puritans: a group of English Christians who settled in Massachusetts to escape persecution in their homeland

Reconstruction: a period after the Civil War when the U.S. government set up new laws and institutions in the South

reservation: a semi-independent territory set up by the U.S. government for Native Americans

segregation: the practice of separating the races in schools, transportation, and public areas

Social Security: a national system of benefits, primarily for retired and disabled people

Trail of Tears: the forced relocation by the U.S. government of five Native American nations in 1838 to western reservations in Oklahoma

Glossary

Selected Bibliography

Boyer, Paul S., ed. *The Oxford Companion to United States History.* New York: Oxford University Press, 2001.
More than 1,400 articles are featured by scholars on the social, political, and economic history of the United States.

Breidlid, Anders, Fredrick Brogger, Oyvind T. Gullikson, and Torbjorn Sirevag, eds. *American Culture: An Anthology of Civilization Texts.* London: Routledge, 1996.
The collection of useful and interesting historical documents touch on many different areas of U.S. history and society.

Corkin, Stanley. *Realism and the Birth of the Modern United States: Cinema, Literature, and Culture.* Athens: University of Georgia Press, 1996.
The author describes how U.S. business and society changed its literature and art around the turn of the twentieth century.

Daniels, Roger, and Otis L. Graham. *Debating American Immigration, 1882–Present.* Lanham, MD: Rowman and Littlefield, 2001.
The collection of essays deals with immigration issues and the debate on the need for closed borders, a central theme of U.S. history.

Edgar, Christopher, and Gary Lenhart. *The Teachers and Writers Guide to Classic American Literature.* New York: Teachers and Writers Collaborative, 2001.
Essays on important American novelists and poets, including African American and women writers, are featured in this book.

The Europa World Year Book 2006. New York: Routledge, 2006.
The article "The United States of America" gives a thorough account of recent history, a statistical database on population and economic trends, and a listing of major government, private industry, and media addresses.

Fox, Richard Wightman, and James T. Kloppenberg. *A Companion to American Thought.* Malden, MA: Blackwell Publishers, 1998.
The collection of articles describes the life and works of leading thinkers in U.S. history, philosophy, literature, politics, and social issues.

Gaile, Gary L., and Cort J. Willmott. *Geography in America at the Dawn of the 21st Century.* New York: Oxford University Press, 2006.
This comprehensive guide to trends in geographical studies includes research in geology and meteorology, environmental studies, resource management, social trends, economics, and ethnic geography.

Garraty, John A., and Eric Foner. *The Readers Companion to American History.* Boston: Houghton Mifflin, 1991.
In a collection of encyclopedia entries and short essays, leading scholars of U.S. history interpret the nation's past and present through major themes such as immigration, religious thought, literature, and political life.

Merchant, Carolyn. *The Columbia Guide to American Environmental History*. New York: Columbia University Press, 2002.
This history of land use and environmental issues throughout the nation's history describes how U.S. society has been affected by its natural surroundings.

Stadelmann, Marcus. *U.S. Presidency for Dummies*. New York: Hungry Minds, 2002.
The book includes basic information and little-known details about all forty-three U.S. presidents and their terms of office.

Suarez-Orozco, Marcelo, and Mariela Paez. *Latinos: Remaking America*. Berkeley: University of California Press, 2002.
The author provides a complete history of Latinos in the United States and a description of how Hispanics are shaping modern U.S. society, business, and politics.

Wood, Andrew F. *Road Trip America: A State-by-State Tour Guide to Offbeat Destinations*. Portland, OR: Collectors Press, 2003.
This search for weird and interesting roadside attractions throughout the country gives much insight into U.S. pop culture in the twentieth century.

Boatner, Mark. *Encyclopedia of the American Revolution.* **Mechanicsburg, PA: Stackpole Books, 1994.**
This handy reference guide to people, events, battles, and key documents of the Revolution is useful to anyone who is researching the topic.

Cott, Nancy F. *No Small Courage: A History of Women in the United States.* **New York: Oxford University Press, 2000.**
The collection of ten essays describes the important role of women throughout U.S. history.

Davis, Kenneth C. *Don't Know Much about the 50 States.* **New York: Harper Trophy, 2001.**
Davis's book of facts, figures, and trivia about each state is packed with interesting and little-known details.

Ellis Island Immigration Museum
http://www.ellisisland.com/
The website is an online exhibit on the history of immigration to the United States and guide to Ellis Island in New York Harbor, where millions of European immigrants first arrived.

Faragher, Jack. *The American Heritage Encyclopedia of American History.* **New York: Henry Holt, 1998.**
This one thousand-plus page book has about three thousand articles covering every aspect of U.S. history, from early explorations to recent social and political issues.

Fifer, Barbara. *Everyday Geography of the United States.* **New York: Black Dog and Leventhal Publishers, 2003.**
This book gives the most important facts about the nation's climate, geography, natural resources, population, and economy.

Finlayson, Reggie. *We Shall Overcome: A History of the American Civil Rights Movement.* **Minneapolis: Twenty-First Century Books, 2003.**
Finlayson provides a history of the fight for equality by African Americans, from the early days of slavery to modern times.

First Gov
http://www.firstgov.gov/
The website offers a handy portal to the entire U.S. government, for researchers and citizens.

Hayes, Derek. *Historical Atlas of the United States.* **Berkeley: University of California Press, 2006.**
Hayes offers a fascinating collection of maps linked to important events and historical trends in the United States.

Josephy, Alvin M., Jr., *500 Nations: An Illustrated History of North American Indians.* **New York: Gramercy Press, 2002.**
The author draws on archaeology, oral history, first-person accounts, official documents and treaties, and other useful sources in a book tied to a public television series on Native American history.

Further Reading and Websites

Library of Congress
http://www.loc.gov/index.html
The site features an online catalog of the largest library in the United States, along with online exhibits, photographs, historical documents, and Thomas, the complete Web guide to U.S. laws and the U.S. Congress.

National Park Service
http://www.nps/gov/
The NPS provides an online tour of all the national parks, plus information on how to visit and explore them.

U.S. Geological Survey
http://www.usgs.gov/
The USGS provides a website about geography, climate, natural resources, and environmental issues in the United States.

vgsbooks.com
http://www.vgsbooks.com
Visit vgsbooks.com, the home page of the Visual Geography Series®. You can get linked to all sorts of useful online information, including geographical, historical, demographic, cultural, and economic websites. The vgsbooks.com site is a great resource for late-breaking news and statistics.

The White House
http://www.whitehouse.gov/
This is the official website of the White House and guide to the policies of the U.S. president.

Whitman, Sylvia, and Trish Marx. *What's Cooking? The History of American Food*. Minneapolis: Twenty-First Century Books, 2001.
An exploration of cooking and food production in the United States, the authors reveal how famous American recipes came to be and cover the debate over modern farming and food engineering.

Zinn, Howard. *People's History of the United States*. New York: Harper Perennial, 2005.
Zinn provides an account of the struggles of Native Americans, African Americans, women, and other minority social and ethnic groups as they face discrimination and persecution throughout the history of the United States.

Captions for photos appearing on cover and chapter openers:

Cover: The Grand Canyon which lies in Arizona was cut by the powerful Colorado River. The canyon has been a national park since 1919.

pp. 4–5 People soak up the sun on a beach in Key West, Florida.

pp. 8–9 The New York City skyline looms over New York Harbor.

pp. 20–21 The Wukoki Pueblo at Wupatki National Monument in Arizona contains more than one hundred rooms. Archaeologists believe ancestors of the Hopi occupied it from about 1100 to 1225.

pp. 36–37 U.S. students of many ethnicities recite the Pledge of Allegiance in their middle-school auditorium in Jericho, Long Island, New York.

pp. 44–45 The Roman Catholic Saint Patrick Cathedral is the oldest continuously used church building in Fort Worth, Texas. It was completed in 1892.

pp. 56–57 Fewer and fewer automotive assembly line jobs, such as this one at the DaimlerChrysler Assembly Plant in Detroit, Michigan, are available in the United States in the twenty-first century.

Photo Acknowledgments
The images in this book are used with the permission of: © Darren Maybury/Art Directors, pp. 4–5; © XNR Productions, pp. 6, 10; © Adina Tovy/Art Directors, pp. 8–9; © Howard Ande, pp. 13, 16, 50 (bottom), 55, 61; Agricultural Research Service, USDA, p. 15; © Peter Robinson/Art Directors, p. 18; © Charles Kogod/National Geographic/Getty Images, pp. 20–21; Library of Congress, pp. 24 (LC-USZC4-2541), 27 (LC-USZ62-1283), 47 (LC-USZ62-56850), 48 (top, LC-USZ62-5513), 48 (bottom, LC-USW3-0302780D); Franklin D. Roosevelt Library, p. 30; © Paul J. Richards/AFP/Getty Images, p. 33; U.S. Coast Guard, p. 34; © Royalty-Free/CORBIS, p. 35; © Dirk Anschutz/Stone/Getty Images, pp. 36–37; Bob Nichols/USDA, p. 38; PhotoDisc Royalty Free by Getty Images, p. 40; © Kevin Fleming/CORBIS, p. 42; © Bob Turner/Art Directors, pp. 44–45; © Independent Picture Service, pp. 46, 50 (top); © Martha Holmes/Time & Life Pictures/Getty Images, p. 49; © Jeff Zelevansky/Icon SMI, p. 52; © Bill Pugliano/Getty Images, pp. 56–57; © Spencer Platt/Getty Images, p. 58; Bureau of Reclamation, p. 60; © Metro Transit, p. 63; © Deborah C. Mink, p. 64, © Brie Cohen/Independent Picture Service, p. 68.

Front Cover: © Tibor Bognar/Art Directors. Back Cover: NASA.